ROCKVILLE CAMPUS LIBRARY

Scientific Attitudes in
Mary Shelley's *Frankenstein*

Studies in Speculative Fiction, No. 8

Robert Scholes, Series Editor

Alumni/Alumnae Professor of English and
Chairman, Department of English
Brown University

Other Titles in This Series

No. 1	*Feminist Futures: Contemporary Women's Speculative Fiction*	Natalie M. Rosinsky
No. 2	*Ray Bradbury and the Poetics of Reverie: Fantasy, Science Fiction, and the Reader*	William F. Touponce
No. 3	*The Scientific World View in Dystopia*	Alexandra Aldridge
No. 4	*Approaches to the Fiction of Ursula K. Le Guin*	James W. Bittner
No. 5	*Utopia: The Psychology of a Cultural Fantasy*	David Bleich
No. 6	*Biological Themes in Modern Science Fiction*	Helen N. Parker
No. 9	*The Novels of Philip K. Dick*	Kim Stanley Robinson
No. 10	*The Politics of Fantasy: C.S. Lewis and J.R.R. Tolkien*	Lee D. Rossi
No. 11	*The Unified Ring: Narrative Art and the Science-Fiction Novel*	Frank Sadler
No. 12	*Science, Myth, and the Fictional Creation of Alien Worlds*	Albert Wendland

Scientific Attitudes in Mary Shelley's *Frankenstein*

by
Samuel Holmes Vasbinder

UMI RESEARCH PRESS
Ann Arbor, Michigan

Copyright © 1984, 1976
Samuel Holmes Vasbinder
All rights reserved

Produced and distributed by
UMI Research Press
an imprint of
University Microfilms International
A Xerox Information Resources Company
Ann Arbor, Michigan 48106

Library of Congress Cataloging in Publication Data

Vasbinder, Samuel Holmes.
  Scientific attitudes in Mary Shelley's *Frankenstein.*

  (Studies in speculative fiction ; no. 8)
  Revision of thesis—Kent State University, 1976.
  Bibliography: p.
  Includes index.
  1. Shelley, Mary Wollstonecraft, 1797-1851.
Frankenstein. 2. Shelley, Mary Wollstonecraft, 1797-1851—
Knowledge—Science. 3. Science in literature. 4. Science—
Great Britain—History—18th century. I. Title. II. Series.
PR5397.F73V3   1984   823'.7   84-8438
ISBN 0-8357-1580-9

To Dr. Donald M. Hassler without whose constant encouragement and help this study would never have been written.

Contents

1 Introduction *1*

2 Mary Shelley and the Critical Tradition *5*

3 The Problem of the Text *31*

4 The Literature on Artificial Humans Prior to 1818 *35*

5 Ceremonial Magic and Alchemy *51*

6 Use of the New Science in *Frankenstein* *65*

7 Conclusion *83*

Notes *85*

Bibliography *103*

Index *109*

1

Introduction

James Rieger's introduction to the 1818 version of *Frankenstein* makes it clear that he believes Mary Shelley knew little science. "*Frankenstein*'s chemistry," he observes, "is switched-on magic, souped-up alchemy, the electrification of Agrippa and Paracelsus." He concludes that "it is a mistake to call *Frankenstein* a pioneer work of science fiction." Even the "technological plausibility that is essential to science fiction" is absent.[1] These statements, as I will point out in the chapter devoted to *Frankenstein* criticism, mirror, with few exceptions, the majority view.

I believe that such an assessment is too hasty and that underlying many of the events of the novel are broad scientific foundations. Carl Grabo has shown that a strong scientific current can be detected in Shelley's *Prometheus Unbound*.[2] Underlying the mythic, symbolic, and poetic language of the poem are layers of scientific learning which had been transformed by Shelley's poetic nature into another form, yet a form in which the original impulses could be recognized as scientific by the trained observer.[3]

With this in mind I began to think that a consideration of *Frankenstein*'s scientific backgrounds carried out in a manner similar to Grabo's treatment of *Prometheus Unbound* might prove fruitful. That despite the vagueness of the scientific data there might prove to be a much deeper scientific base upholding the story itself, a base that would enable it to be built in scientific terms without the suffocation of heavy layers of science.

A subsequent analysis of this scientific background has indeed shown that Mary did not write the book in a vacuum; that alchemy and sorcery figure as little in the novel as supernatural elements do; and that science, in the eighteenth-century sense of the term is, while very low profile, nevertheless pervasive. It is very easy to miss this scientific aspect of the novel. Unless the critic is well acquainted with the scientific matters of the age much of the science that forms the basis of *Frankenstein* will remain invisible.

It will be the purpose of this study to make the scientific background more visible. The following method will be used. First, I will examine the criticism the book has generated in the last 150 years and demonstrate that the science aspect has in general been overlooked in favor of the moral fable. Second, I will review the matter of the text and advance reasons for the use of the first edition of *Frankenstein* as the major source of information for this investigation, with the manuscript and the final, edited version of 1831 being used where needed. Third, I will present the history of the artificial man in the literature of Western civilization and contrast the artificial man in *Frankenstein* with the species in general. Fourth, I will examine the novel in detail to determine if ceremonial magic and alchemy play as large a part in the story as Rieger asserts, and demonstrate that both of these elements are almost absent. Fifth, I will present the scientific echoes and materials contained in the novel to justify my assertion that the novel is at its base built on the monistic, Newtonian science of Erasmus Darwin, Joseph Priestley, and Sir Humphry Davy.

These points, analyzed in detail, will indicate that surrounding the novel is a strong scientific atmosphere which cannot be ignored and which provides needed meaning. The analysis will define the strongly scientific nature of the novel and help place it well within the tradition of speculative fiction.

Since the term "speculative fiction" is one I will frequently use, it must be defined. Speculative fiction is a term more comprehensive than the earlier, more well-known "science fiction." The term, whose exact origin is in dispute, is often attributed to Robert A. Heinlein who employed it in an address given at the 1933 World Science Fiction Convention.[4] The term has in the last few years gained currency, and, because it implies a more comprehensive description of the genre that Mary Shelley was working in when she produced *Frankenstein,* I prefer to use it.

Basically, it refers to those works that have a scientific or pseudo-scientific base, whose stories are set in hypothetical, future societies or which make use of newly created, technological advances that cause radical change or distress in the environment into which they are introduced. Consequently, the areas into which speculative fiction can enter successfully are not easily definable.

By its very nature speculative fiction, whose life is its powerful, imaginative spirit, assumes a protean shape. As a result the themes used are often so superimposed, or the ideas presented by a variety of speculative fiction novels are so different, that each critic, reader, and writer can set his own personal parameters. I do not believe, however, that *Frankenstein* is a work that can be left out of the genre. Mary Shelley preserves a strong scientific tone at the very outset in the Arctic letters of the English scientist, Robert Walton. This scientific tone is maintained throughout great portions of the novel, but has to date been regarded as pseudoscience with no real connection to eighteenth-century science, or has been ignored as a peripheral issue.

I would like to make it clear at the outset that I realize *Frankenstein* is a complex novel that can be viewed from a number of critical angles, many of which have a validity of their own. I do not want to claim that my interpretation is the only acceptable reading and that all other evaluations have falsified the novel's message. It is my hope that this study presents enough evidence to show that the scientific aspects of *Frankenstein* have a legitimacy of their own and must be considered as much an integral part of the novel as the Miltonic echoes on the moral fable.

2
Mary Shelley and the Critical Tradition

Frankenstein has generated a considerable body of criticism since its publication in 1818.[1] This has, in the main, concerned itself with four ideas: the Gothic base of horror upon which the story is laid; the Promethean, Miltonic, and Faustian motifs present throughout the book; the peripheral literature that seems to have offered a creative impulse to the story; and the biographical element of the novel which sees Frankenstein, the Monster, and Henry Clerval as the alter egos of Shelley. Because critics often discuss several of these points in a single article, it will be easiest to describe the criticism in chronological order.

The first criticisms of the book, reflected in the reviews written at the time of first publication, are revealing because (with the exception of *Blackwood's Edinburgh Magazine*) they adopted attitudes that remained unchanged well into the twentieth century.[2] With the exception of a few critics, modern evaluations have altered little in essential attitudes. Of the leading literary magazines in Mary's time, four reviewed the book.

Blackwood's Edinburgh Magazine was the only literary review of its time that endorsed the ideas upon which the novel was based.[3] It prefaced the actual criticism of *Frankenstein* with a long essay discussing "the class of marvellous romances" into which it saw this novel clearly fitting. It calls the author "a person of uncommon powers of poetic imagination." *Blackwood's* does not shrink from praising the author's style "written in plain and forcible English without exhibiting that mixture of hyperbolical Germanisms with which tales of wonder are usually told." In this judgment *Blackwood's* concurred with the other reviews that all felt the writer was a gifted person. The review noted that "upon the whole, the work impresses us with a high idea of the author's original genius and happy power of expression," and went on to "congratulate our readers upon a novel which excites new reflections and untried sources of emotion." *Blackwood's* is the only magazine that gave a review of the novel entirely free of antagonistic comment. The *Edinburgh Magazine*'s comments put the book in an entirely different light.

The *Edinburgh Magazine* devoted five pages to *Frankenstein*.[4] They admitted that the novel possessed "a . . . power of fascination" and "a harsh and savage delineation of power." They further conceded that this effect of terror was "relieved by the gentler features of domestic and simple feeling" which the book contained in abundance. Beyond these concessions, their final judgment was unfavorable.

> It is one of those works, however, which when we read, we do not well see why it should have been written; for a *jeu d'esprit* it is somewhat too long, grave and laborious, and some of our highest and most reverential feelings receive a shock from the conception upon which it turns so as to produce a painful and bewildered state of mind while we peruse it.[5]

The *Gentleman's Magazine* also expressed much the same view.

> This tale is evidently the production of no ordinary Writer; and though we are shocked at the idea of the event on which the fiction is founded, many parts of it are strikingly good, and the description of scenery is excellent.

Note that it is the everyday scene that is praised but that the very basis of the novel is ignored as being too "shocking" to be seriously appraised.

Another review of *Frankenstein* was published by *La Belle Assemblée*, a magazine for upper-class ladies, whose articles revolved around fashion, society news, and reviews of popular plays and belles lettres.[6] The bulk of the review is devoted to a recapitulation of the plot. It is prefaced by a short, two-paragraph evaluation of the purpose of the story. The review found it a "very bold fiction," which if it were not for the statement in the novel's preface, he would find "impious." The reviewer hopes that the writer of the novel had a "moral view" in mind, one that will show clearly "that the presumptive works of man must be frightful, vile, and horrible; ending only in discomfort and misery to himself." The review is not in the least intellectual and repeats what is later to become one of the most common, superficial comments made on the novel.

But it was the *Quarterly Review* that attacked the novel most strenuously. Partially because of the feud they were then carrying on with Shelley, and partially because the book was dedicated to Godwinian ideals, they suspected that the anonymously printed book was the work of Shelley himself and treated it accordingly to the most scathing abuse. After presenting a resumé of the plot, the *Quarterly* proceeded to deliver its opinion, an opinion that constitutes the most savage attack the novel had sustained.

> But when we have thus admitted that *Frankenstein* has passages which appal the mind and make the flesh creep, we have given it all the praise (if praise it can be called) which we dare to bestow. Our taste and our judgment alike revolt at this kind of writing, and the greater the ability with which it may be executed the worse it is—it inculcates no lesson of conduct, manners, or morality; it cannot mend, and will not even amuse its readers, unless their taste have been deplorably vitiated—it fatigues the feelings without interesting the understanding; it gratuitously harasses the heart, and wantonly adds to the store, already too great, of painful sensations.[7]

Although their comments are more polite and detached than the *Quarterly Review*'s, modern critics have often arrived at the same conclusion. The very things that "appal the mind" of the *Quarterly*'s reviewer find very modern support. It will become clear that while the didacticism of *Frankenstein* and the literary and classical learning of Mary are exhaustively treated and approved of, the heart of the book, the creation of the monster by scientific methods, is often felt to be in the way as an embarrassment. No one has made a serious attempt to expose the scientific learning present in the novel, preferring to believe that Mary picked up detached pieces of scientific gossip and was able to miraculously piece them together into a coherent whole. The science of the book was brought in, so many believe, only to present a picture of the evils of knowledge and to demonstrate the punishment that awaited all those who dared aspire to divine matters. This view is held by many critics of speculative fiction in general. Until recently the genre was held to be the product of enthusiastic but uninformed writers who warped science to suit their own purposes and, as such, produced fiction that was merely frivolous and wrong-headed. Critic after critic will give evidence of this tendency, which began with the earliest reviews of *Frankenstein*.

After the contemporary reviews, the critics are silent until the first biography of Mary Shelley was brought out in 1886.[8] Written by Helen Moore, the book devoted a long chapter to *Frankenstein*. The biography is slanted to a popular audience and makes no pretence of being scholarly, although the facts presented are, for the most part, accurate. In comparison with the best, most readable biography of Mary written by R. Glynn Grylls in 1938, this life of Mary is extremely short. But despite the brevity, Moore's biographical study begins to repeat what will become the usual statements about the life of Mary, the origins of the novel, and the lesson it is supposed to teach the reader.

The chapter that discusses *Frankenstein* notes first that the novel has a long history of being able to interest both a mass readership and the littérateur. She spends some time discussing the origin of the novel, as revealed by Mary in the 1831 introduction, repeating all of the commonplace beliefs that the book was inspired by the Shelley-Byron conversations and that Mary contributed nothing to the book except the central figures. "Nothing," she observes, "could be simpler than the plot, nothing more horrible than the situation and details." After giving the briefest resumé of the plot, she begins to discuss the manner in which this novel differs from the average "fantastic romance." She discovers that the work is "utterly different" from anything then written in the Gothic Style. She believes that the great hold the novel has exercised over the minds of readers can be attributed to its prophetic element. "It is by virtue of the allegorical element in it," she asserts, "that it holds its high position as a work of the imagination." Mrs. Moore believes that Mary was aware of this element when she gave the book its double title, and that this idea is further reinforced when one considers that "the stories which suggested it were all weird in form and allegorical in type." The rest of her discussion focuses on the manner in which the allegory is worked out, chiefly the idea that there is "a tendency in the human being to discard the established order of things and to create for itself a new and independent existence." It is noteworthy that Helen Moore rejects the idea that the book is simply a Gothic horror story, realizing that the novel possessed complexities which had not as yet been adequately determined.

In 1889 Mrs. Julian Marshall published a two-volume biography based upon the known letters and journals of the Shelley circle.[9] It was the first attempt to gather the scattered personal papers dealing with the life of Mary Shelley alone, and present this material along with a running commentary that served as a narrative focus. She says little about *Frankenstein* beyond the usual, well-known biographical statements. *Frankenstein* is mentioned only when it assumes importance as an event in Mary's daily life. Mrs. Marshall does not offer any critical estimate of the book.

A second biography of Mary Shelley was published in 1890, written by Lucy Maddox Rossetti.[10] It is a short, sentimental view, pedestrian and unscholarly. She devotes an entire chapter to *Frankenstein* but confines herself mainly to retelling the plot without comment. She does point out that Mary does not simply "depict the horror of such a monster." Rossetti sees that she also:

> wished to show what a being, with no naturally bad propensities might sink to when under the influence of a false position—the education of Rousseau's natural man not being here possible.

Richard Garnett, the eminent nineteenth-century critic and commentator, was the first to collect all of Mary's shorter works of fiction into one book.[11] It remains the only complete collection of her short works in existence. In his introduction to this work, Garnett discusses *Frankenstein* at some length. He believes that while Mary's original intention was to "paint Frankenstein's monstrous creation as an object of unmitigated horror," another concern also underlies the book: "The perception that he [the artificial man] was an object of intimate compassion." This preoccupation with moral responsibilities remains the most often mentioned aspect of the novel.

The range of nineteenth-century criticism, then, takes note of several properties of the novel that continue to be noticed and expanded upon in the criticism of the twentieth century. The early reviews judge the scientific themes as unworthy of a writer but pay tribute to Mary's powerful writing ability, misplaced as they deem it to be, perceiving in the novel something beyond the ordinary. The biographical works that followed also take note of the book's strong symbolic bias and begin to notice the handling of evil and the responsibility of the scientist to his creations, themes which will be extensively examined in twentieth-century criticism.

In 1921 the first assessment of the weird tale as a legitimate art form was published, containing a great deal of attention to *Frankenstein*.[12] Edith Birkhead's book, *The Tale of Terror,* is the first serious attempt to categorize types of horror fiction, and along the way analyzes all the well-known novels of the genre as well as many lesser-known works of terror fiction. Birkhead notes the debt Mary owed to the Gothic tradition.

> It is evident from the records of her reading that the novel of terror in all its guises was familiar to her. She had beheld the majestic horror of the halls of Eblis; she had threaded her way through Mrs. Radcliffe's artfully constructed Gothic castles; she had braved the terrors of the German Ritter-Rauber-und Schauer-Romane; she had assisted, fearful, at Lewis's midnight diablerie; she had patiently unravelled the "mystery" novels of Godwin and of Charles Brockden Brown.

Mary chose not to adopt all of the paraphernalia of the Gothic horror story. She dispensed with "the shrieking chorus of malevolent abbesses, diabolical monks, intriguing marquises, Wandering Jews and bleeding spectres" that were so familiar to readers of that genre. These had been "grievously overworked in previous performances" and Mary, in trying to imitate but not copy, discovered how to elicit horror without recourse to all of these standard props. She succeeded in doing this in a way "completely her own." But despite this innovation *Frankenstein* fails for Birkhead because it "is obviously the work of an immature writer who has had no experience in evolving a plot." Evidently Birkhead bases her idea of the weakness of plot on Mary's unwillingness to write a story that was Gothic in the purest sense of the word, preferring to innovate upon the theme.

Birkhead clearly perceives that Mary "is weighted down by commonsense," but as a critic Birkhead does not ask herself why this might be so. *Frankenstein* fails to meet all the criteria of Gothicism and must, for Birkhead at least, be judged faulty. Mary "flutters instead of soaring, unwilling to trust herself far from the material world," a fact that in itself cannot fail to make a strong case for a scientific view of the work. But for Birkhead the science is largely unnecessary.

> By resting her terrors on a pseudo-scientific basis and by placing her story in a definite locality, Mrs. Shelley waives her right to entire suspension of disbelief.

In other words, the book should fit the mould of the horror tale but does not; it is necessary to make excuses for its Gothic deficiencies rather than examine the text from a point of view that does not demand supernatural explanations at all points. Yet even with all of these faults, it "still has power momentarily 'to make the reader dread to look around, to curdle the blood, and to quicken the beatings of the heart.' " The book is still Gothic, still in the tradition of the horror story. No mention is made of the scientific strivings of Victor for the secret of the vital spark. In fact, this early life of Victor is judged to be "tedious and largely unnecessary." For Birkhead, the success of *Frankenstein* hinges on the later exposition of the monster's life. As such it becomes "a plea for human sympathy" and "dwells on the pathos of ugliness and deformity," ultimately giving Mary's creation a "dual nature that prevents him from being a mere automaton."

A second commentator on the horror story, Eino Railo, compiled an extensive evaluation of this type of fiction similar to that of Birkhead but on an enlarged scale. In this work, called *The Haunted Castle,* he clearly points out that Mary did not make herself subservient to the Gothic tradition in all ways, but he does little to investigate the direction she does take.[13] He notes that Mary "breaks away from the traditional haunted castle and chooses as her chief character a young scientist who succeeds . . . in extending the bounds of human knowledge." However, he does point out that the scientific atmosphere of the book is pervasive and needs to be considered, although he does not have the room to expand upon his observations. But this science is really alchemy mixed with sorcery, not empirical, Newtonian science.

Railo notes that "the haunted room" has become a "cabbalistic laboratory, where the bounds of knowledge are shattered and spirit solves the basic problems of existence." It is significant that the laboratory is still discussed in occult terms. It is not the workroom of a man obsessed with the new science, but still has overtones of the necromantic inquirer after knowledge. True, Victor's attic room is in many ways the extension of an alchemist's laboratory. But it differs in many important ways also, none of which Railo investigates. For him:

> the cabbalism of earlier romanticism is the forerunner of the "science" of a later generation, and leads gradually to the use of scientific-looking methods and the kinds of mysteries to which the method lends itself.[14]

Railo's quotation marks around "science" indicate that for him Frankenstein's research is still magic and sorcery. Yet the methods of investigation Victor uses are strongly Newtonian, not just "scientific-looking." Railo further compares Victor's laboratory to Manfred's mountain retreat, calling it "a typical haunted castle." The "tower room" of this place is fitted out to represent an alchemist's laboratory which must be evaluated as "a stage of mystical powers, Faust's chamber, the former laboratory of alchemists and sorcerers." For Railo, Mary's employment of science and its methods is only a method of "supporting a romantic plot," a method which has "proved exceedingly fertile in later romanticism." His final estimate of the story is that it fails to really satisfy the requirements of the Gothic horror story. "The final impression," he observes, "is that the author has sought to air her opinions on the duties of society towards the poor, particularly as regards sympathy and education."

Both Birkhead and Railo represent the earlier type of criticism, traditional and in some respects justified, that the story must be viewed solely as an attempt to write a horror story in the Walpole/Lewis vein. This attempt largely fails because Mary does not apply the accepted techniques of the Gothic thriller to *Frankenstein*. She is guilty of too much innovation.

Richard Church's biography is a workmanlike but short study more concerned with pretty turns of phrase than scholarly completeness.[15] He refers to *Frankenstein* as a "sinister flower." Church recounts the often-rehearsed details of the *Frankenstein* origin. He considers the book "an adolescent's version of the eternal story of Man's attempt to create human life," but admits that in spite of the faults of brevity and clumsiness of plot it "must be considered . . . a permanent addition to the world's literature of the macabre." He believes that Mary indulges herself in mental self-torture and that the composition of *Frankenstein* allowed her to wallow in some of the more wretched moments of her life. He points particularly to the child named William the monster kills, and since it bears the name of Mary's own dead baby, Church regards the episode as one of several essays in self-pity with which the novel is supplied. In other words "she made the book a battleground for her own unreconciled emotional and intellectual struggles." Church adds nothing to the *Frankenstein* criticism beyond this.

R. Glynn Grylls, Lady Manders, wrote the first scholarly biography of Mary.[16] Except for a few small errors of fact, it remains today one of the most important sources of commentary on the novelist's life and provides a studious estimate of her writing. Grylls does little, however, to offer a critical view of *Frankenstein,* confining herself to a history of the book's origin and publication, a summary of contemporary reviews of the novel, and a lengthy summary of the plot. Her only critical comment on the novel is that "the importance [of *Frankenstein*] in the history of the novel depends primarily on the originality of the plot and on the descendents for which it has been responsible."[17]

Milton Millhauser's article on *Frankenstein* offers a clue to an important secondary theme of the novel that had never before been commented upon.[18] He sees that coincidental with the story is a "thin veil of social speculation" which is "stereotyped and irrelevant," speculation which mindlessly repeats the Godwinian lessons Mary had absorbed from her father. He analyzes at some length the education of the monster as it applies to that brand of radical liberalism he believes Mary tried to explore using the novel as her medium. Millhauser's arguments will be discussed at greater length in reference to the monster's psychology.

In 1951 Muriel Spark, now a well-known critic of Mary Shelley, attempted a biographical reassessment including a chapter on *Frankenstein.*[19] She applies the term "Gothic" to the novel as a "loose definition," adding that the novel is "the first of a new and hybrid species." Spark mentions that the "raw materials" of the novel were "ultimately combined." These were "the supernatural and the harrowing" and, "specifically," the "scientific proposition." She becomes the first critic to refuse to back away from the scientific aspect of the novel, regarding it as a necessary ingredient to a story of this nature. She goes on to analyze the "motif of revolt" represented by the Promethean reference in the title. She also discusses the reception the novel had in the hands of the critics, its style, and modern assessments besides her own. But her work is chiefly interesting for strenuously arguing that the main characters are the doppelgängers of Shelley and that to a large extent the novel is strongly autobiographical, a view she shares with Richard Church. Most critics believe that Spark fails to establish this point with any certainty, but her biographical assessment of Mary remains one of the works to consider in any critical view of the novelist. Some of her views were published at the same time in the British Broadcasting Company's semi-intellectual magazine *The Listener.*

Spark evaluates the novel as "the glorification of man by man carried to its rational extreme."²⁰ She correctly notes that while "the horror of Gothicism is there" it does not have any of Gothicism's "supernatural devices." It is, like Mary's novel *The Last Man,* "a blend of horror and realism." Spark asserts that it must be a novel of "scientific speculation" and that it is prophetic in its ultimate message concerning man's relationship to the acquisition of knowledge, and the things brought into being out of that knowledge. Mary's story "culminates in the romantic motif of man in search of himself and in conflict with himself." The final judgment of Mary and *Frankenstein* is that "she was not a great novelist; she was not artist enough to be considered one." The novel's interest and claim to continuing publication lies in Mary's "macabre inventiveness," as well as the "rational turn of mind" that gives her greatness.

Lewis Awad contributes a very interesting article on the android— or man-made man—in literature, concentrating most of his article on *Frankenstein.*²¹ He sees the monster as the leading type of its kind and one of the most outstanding androids in the history of literature. In his lengthy historical summary of the android, Awad ranges over Oriental and European literature, ancient and modern, to show how common is the idea of man-made men. But his analysis of *Frankenstein* concerns itself more with Percy Shelley's science than with the novel itself. It is almost as if he sees Shelley as the author of *Frankenstein,* not Mary. Mr. Awad's lengthy and scholarly information on the artificial man will be referred to in discussing the precursors of the monster, and the alchemist strain in the novel.

Elizabeth Nitchie's biography of Mary Shelley is indispensable, and remains the single best source of critical evaluation and correct biographical information available.²² Cooly observant, never frantic or sentimental about her subject, she makes some interesting remarks on *Frankenstein.* She is the first biographer to give Mary credit for her scientific learning, a learning based on an accurate knowledge of Newton's empirical method.

> No young woman could have written so effectively of Frankenstein's scientific curiosity unless she had shared it to some degree. Absorbing from her reading (she had read Davy in October, 1816, while she was at work on *Frankenstein*) and from the conversation of Shelley some sense of what it meant to think at the same time scientifically and imaginatively, Mary set her lively mind to work on the possible results of research into the mystery of the life principle.²³

It is most unfortunate that Nitchie's discussion of the science ends with this short account because she must have a great deal more insight to offer into the matter. She spends much time discussing the scientific backgrounds of Mary's novel *The Last Man,* analyzing the science of this work. Her remarks on *Frankenstein* are scattered throughout the book and summarize most of what has been mentioned by earlier commentators.

M. A. Goldberg's article discusses moral responsibility in *Frankenstein,* developing at length an idea that had been tentatively considered by the earlier critics.[24] Goldberg explores the dimensions of the moral difficulty faced by Victor as he first turns his back on his creation and then, realizing his personal liability, attempts to destroy his creation. Goldberg first takes up the moral context as it is felt at the outset of the story. He maintains that Victor tells his history to Walton as a kind of "exemplum" aimed at "weaning" the fellow scientist from his "obsession." Goldberg discusses how this opening motif, i.e., "the temptation and the punishment," as well as "the estrangement," is worked out consistently in the novel. For Goldberg the monster is a weight of guilt, similar to the Ancient Mariner's albatross. It is a punishment meted out by a just Heaven for Victor daring to transgress into the field of forbidden knowledge. Goldberg then moves to a consideration of the Miltonic and Promethean parallels, and concludes his discussion by noting that the moral of the book is aimed at depicting the loneliness of man in "the social and moral context of the nineteenth century England."

I will not summarize Eileen Biglund's biography.[25] It is simply another life, well-written and comprehensive, but it adds nothing to the critical history that has not already been said. She sees *Frankenstein* as others have, an allegorical rendering of the evil implicit in man's life.

Lowry Nelson's "Night Thoughts on the Gothic Novel" calls attention to *Frankenstein* as speculative fiction.[26] He explains that the novel is "more nearly an example of science fiction." The main theme, he believes, is "the good-bad nature of man, echoing what others have said." Mary's most "striking achievement" is "the creation of universal symbolic significance in a narrative that on the surface lays claim to utter oddity and uniqueness." He discusses Victor's guilt, the Promethean sources, and the Miltonic echoes, ending his essay with a lengthy discussion of the manner in which *Frankenstein* and Matthew G. Lewis's novel *The Monk* take on "symbolic resonance." It is unfortunate that while perceiving that *Frankenstein* is indeed science fiction, he fails to develop the idea beyond the barest outlines.

James Rieger's article "Dr. Polidori and the Genesis of *Frankenstein*" is an important addition to the scholarly literature on the novel.[27] It is one of the first articles to shed new light on *Frankenstein* by opening a fresh vein of speculation concerning the creative genesis of the story. He immediately calls into question the accepted version of the origin of the novel as it is told in Mary's introduction of 1832. He maintains that when Mary indicates she is a bit hazy about the details we can infer that "she remembers nothing." Rieger painstakingly traces the probable course of events by going to the sources Mary mentions in order to compare her "faulty" memory with the works she alludes to themselves. The book of ghost stories she remembers and from which she limns the faint outline of the stories was entitled *Fantasmagoriana, ou Recueil d'Histoires d'Apparitions de Spectres, Revenans, Fantômes, etc; traduit de l'allemend, par un Amateur* (Paris, 1812). Rieger indicates the specific titles of the stories Mary remembers in vague detail and presents short reviews of the actual story beside the story as Mary recalls it in her introduction. The "History of the Inconstant Lover" is actually "La Morte Fiancée," while the story about "the tale of the sinful founder of his race" is "Les Portraits de Famille."[28] The crux of Rieger's argument rests on Mary's lapses of memory. If she is inaccurate on some points, she may be inaccurate in others.

> None of this would be of the slightest importance, were it not that Mary Shelley insists so positively upon the accuracy of her memory. If Italian noblemen have sexual intercourse with the wrong ghosts, and Hamlet's father does not stamp along corridors with the beaver up, what credit can there be for the skull-headed lady?

One of the reasons for these facts being overlooked is the "extreme rarity of the *Fantasmagoriana*." Only one scholar is on record as having read it—Polidori's editor and biographer, W. M. Rossetti—who pronounced it "a poor sort of book." Rieger then dissects the situation as Mary Shelley records the sequence. By comparing notes, he finds that Polidori's records of the event are more reliable than Mary's. This fact is difficult to accept on face value, despite Rieger's piece of conclusive evidence that proves Polidori's veracity, i.e., Polidori's dissertation *De Oneirodynia* published the year before. As an expert on sleepwalking, then, Polidori would have been a person Percy Shelley could have (and did) hold many conversations with. Further, Polidori was a "first-rate" physician, "fresh out of Edinburgh." Rieger believes that, unlike Mary who only sat and listened, Polidori would have had an important part in the conversation and "held up his own end." In matters of science, the kind of matters being discussed in daily conversations, Polidori was "perforce an expert," and recognized as such by the Shelley circle.

The importance of all these facts, Rieger believes, "is that it shifts critical emphasis with regard to *Frankenstein*," enabling us for the first time to see this novel "totally divorced from and unembarrassed by the Gothic tradition." This is not to say that the Miltonic echoes and other parallels with literature are not present, but it makes possible the scholarly evaluation of the novel as a book written on other bases, as will be shown. Although Rieger only grudgingly admits that *Frankenstein* is speculative fiction ("It can vulgarly be called science fiction . . ."), he sees the book as a work of "anti-humanist morality quite exempt . . . from the disadvantages of a mere tale of spectres and enchantment." He opens the work up to evaluation on bases other than Gothic, supernatural criteria, criteria which he clearly shows do not apply to this work as exactly as former critics such as Birkhead would have liked.

Mary Graham Lund contributed two articles to the scholarly material written about *Frankenstein*. The first, "Mary Godwin Shelley and the Monster," is a fictional reconstruction of Mary's life and the elements in it that might have had some influence on the genesis of the novel.[29] The article rehearses all the clichés about the book and wonders in little-girl manner about the dreamy, vague hours of Mary's childhood that culminate in her creation of the monster. The article is not scholarly in its approach and adds nothing of value to the canon of scholarship. It is written in much the same manner as a historical novel, recreating situations that might or might not have happened.

Lund's second article is more workmanlike, comparing Shelley directly to Frankenstein.[30] For Lund, *Frankenstein* "is Mary Godwin's own story of her tragic love, of her suprahuman poet lover." For Lund this is the "deep truth" of *Frankenstein*. The novel must be read as a fictional expression of deep-seated, psychological forces. The novel gains its main thrust from the autobiographical and biographical material which Lund reads into it. Certainly all of Mary Shelley's works have an autobiographical element; but to claim that the whole truth rests on one aspect of creativity seems an absurd proposition, especially for a novel that has such a rich and varied background.

The English critics R. E. Douse and D. J. Palmer are co-editors of the Everyman edition of *Frankenstein*. Their introduction to this edition of *Frankenstein* agrees in part with Spark's estimate: "The strength of her story lies in its imaginative vision, not in the overt didacticism with which she overlays it."[31] But in both of these critics, the novel goes beyond this view. They see it as a blend of "modern scientific investigation with the mystic inspiration of medieval alchemy." This idea elaborates the "central fable" of the book "man's desire to understand and control himself," an idea that echoes a number of commentators. This "attempt to rationalize the supernatural" is vital to the meaning of the book for these two critics. The scientist is seen, therefore, as a man who unleashes evil of a very high caliber upon the world. This evil has "no autonomous existence of its own, independent of the human life upon which it preys." It is, of necessity, "a distortion of human nature."

Mary's use of "awesome physical circumstances" whether geographical, physiological or mental provides "merely stage settings for inner revelation."

The distinguished critic Harold Bloom provides an important essay in Mary Shelley criticism.[32] His article was first placed as the afterword to the Signet edition of *Frankenstein* published by the New American Library. As such it serves to summarize and comment upon much of the criticism which had been written up to that time. He calls attention to the Adamic overtones of the monster and the Miltonic parallels of the book. For Bloom the true meaning of the work is embodied by the monster and the insight into his personality that Mary Shelley evokes.

> If we stand back from Mary Shelley's novel in order better to view its archetypal shape, we see it as the quest of a solitary and ravaged consciousness first for consolation, then for revenge, and finally for a self-destruction that will be apocalyptic, that will bring down the creator with his creature.

He calls attention here to the old note sounded so often, that man will destroy himself if he meddles with knowledge beyond his ability to understand.

> Though Mary Shelley may not have intended it, her novel's prime theme is a necessary counterpoise to Prometheanism, for Prometheanism exalts the increase in consciousness despite all cost. Frankenstein breaks through the barrier that separates man from God, and apparently becomes the giver of life, but all he actually can give is death-in-life.

Bloom sees the novel as a forecast of doom, a doom that is inevitable when men meddle in affairs beyond their competencies and abilities. Bloom believes that a fitting epigraph for *Frankenstein* is the Fury's awful taunt to Prometheus where he lies "crucified on his icy Precipice." "All best things," shrieks the Fury, "are thus confused to ill."

In another important article, Burton R. Pollin discusses more literary analogues of *Frankenstein*.[33] He sees that the derivation of the story goes deeper than the simple origins alluded to in Mary's introduction to the novel and Shelley's preface. Pollin points out the story's debt to the following sources: Ovid's *Metamorphoses,* Milton's *Paradise Lost,* Locke's *Essay Concerning Human Understanding, Pygmalion et Galatée*—a play by Mme. de Genlis, and assorted essays by Condillac and Diderot. He further observes that what was originally begun as "a short tale" was to be developed "at greater length" at Shelley's insistence:

> This more ambitious endeavor required an assortment of materials for her novel which go much further back, in their provenance, than the nightmare of the "pale student

of unhallowed arts kneeling beside the thing he had put together . . . the hideous phantasm of a man stretched out."

Pollin believes that the play by Stéphanie Félicité Ducrest de Saint-Aubin, Marquise de Sillery and Comptesse de Genlis represents an important source of the android of Frankenstein. Mary had read the *Nouveaux Nouvelles* which "consist of varied types of diction, including novellas, short stories, and a few dramatic sketches," the most important of which is the play entitled *Pygmalion et Galatée: ou La Statue animée depuis vingt-quatre heures*. Pollin "assumes" that Mary read this story, sometime before the nightmare she experienced, and that the "ideas of injustice of the world . . . slaves . . . tyranny . . . the extremes of poverty and wealth, hunting, and deception" all have a profound affect on Mary's creative instincts as the idea for her own novel takes shape. There is little doubt that Mme. de Genlis' drama aroused in Mary the memories of Ovid's *Metamorphoses* which "she had laboriously been construing under Shelley's tutelage only a year before." The connection between the beautiful Galatée and the hideous monster constructed by Victor exist only in their miraculous animation. Under the hand of a mortal scientist that android is infused with the spirit of life while the shaped marble of Pygmalion's statue breathes under the influence of a divine fiat given by Venus.

Another important source was Milton's *Paradise Lost,* attention to which is brought to bear in the epigraph to the novel from *Paradise Lost,* Book X, lines 743–45.

> Did I request thee, Maker, from my clay
> To mould me man? Did I solicit thee
> From darkness to promote me?

Pollin isolates three themes from *Paradise Lost* that he feels are implicit in the novel itself: "the molding of a living being 'from clay,' the growth of malice and the desire for revenge, and the isolation of this hostile being and the consequent increase of this hostility." For Pollin, these facts elicit the judgment that "the spirit of Milton's work permeates Mary Shelley's work, from the title page until almost the very end." One of Pollin's most important contributions to the study of Mary's novel is his isolation of the Miltonic echoes presented by the book. This paragraph illuminates one of Mary's major sources:

> Mary Shelley refers to the Faustian idea that knowledge intoxicates and is dangerous when excessive (pp. 17, 46, 49), becoming a serpent's "sting" in itself (p. 19) or in its product (p. 179). Frankenstein hopes to be blessed as the "source" of a "new species"

(p. 47), but ironically his product evolves into a self-acknowledged Satan (pp. 136, 143, 229), who swears eternal revenge upon his creator and all the human race (pp. 150, 204). The monster himself reflects that Hell is an internal condition (pp. 53, 88, 220) which is intensified, if not produced, through loneliness (pp. 125, 156). His only salvation in the face of universal ostracism is a mate, to be created by Frankenstein as his "Eve" (p. 156). His culminating nature follows upon the destruction of this requested second weird creation by the scientist himself, fearful lest a stranger, malevolent race may dominate mankind (pp. 176–177).[34]

Through these strong Miltonic echoes, Pollin draws attention to the image of the animated statue, a figure that "has become almost a metaphorical cliché among the Encyclopaedists and their English followers." This figure is used to illustrate the "whole development of perception and of complex and abstract ideas" set forth by Condillac in his *Traité du sensations* (1754). Pollin believes that Condillac's philosophy and writings "were likely to be cited in the Diodati discussions and are a probable artistic source of the novel."

Diderot too, because of his close associations with Condillac, offers another possible source of the novel. Pollin points out that Shelley was familiar with Diderot's *Lettre sur les sourds et muets,* a work often thought to have suggested the "statue device to Condillac." Further, Mary confides in her journal that at the period she was doing her initial thinking on *Frankenstein,* she was reading Diderot's *Tableau de famille* which helped to "indirectly" shape the work. Pollin also observes that Diderot's *Lettre sur les aveugles,* with its speculation on the manner in which human consciousness begins to function, is analogous to the dawning of the android's sensations in the weeks immediately following his creation. Diderot is seen linked to Locke, upon whose *Essay Concerning Human Understanding* Mary "spent an unusual amount of time," nearly a month and a half. Pollin asserts she got certain "underlying assumptions" from him, particularly:

> the absence of innate principles, the derivation of all ideas from sensation or reflection, and the efficacy of pleasure and pain in causing us to seek or avoid the various objects of sensation.

Pollin, therefore, calls our attention not only to certain literary analogues of *Frankenstein*'s genesis and a variety of minor works which can be linked to the novel, but he also points out for the first time the importance of sensationalist theory as a strong intellectual force in the shaping of this book. He perceives accurately the importance of Condillac's statue as a counterpart for Mary Shelley's artificial man and assesses the impact other materialists such as Diderot and Locke may have had on Mary's creative thought. I will point out at greater length in a subsequent chapter a number of other implications the sensationalist theories have in the novel and attempt to show how they are utilized, particularly in the first days of the artificial man's existence.

Although Stephen Crafts was an undergraduate when he wrote his essay on *Frankenstein,* it is worth considering.[35] The university periodical in which it appeared was specifically geared to consider political revolution of the most radical type and offers a curious twentieth-century parallel to the political radicalism of the Romantics. It seems almost natural that a novel such as *Frankenstein* would appeal to such a group. For Crafts, Mary Shelley "explores metaphorically the usurpation of sensibility by intellect and the concomitant human relationships the perversion produces." He sees that the insane actions of Frankenstein's android

> are not those of an inherently evil creature but the desperate gropings of a sensitive being attempting to assert a form of humanity following its objectification within a technological concept.

Such a statement is used to indicate how *Frankenstein* represents symbolically the attempt of "industrial societies to stifle human sensibility within the all-inclusive context of abstraction." Crafts sees the novel as a parable for our own times in which man, utilizing science to satisfy his own egocentricities, finds that his creation recoils upon him and seeks to destroy its maker. The monster also represents huge sections of society that are sacrificed on the altar of economic production or colonial empire in order to satisfy the needs of a powerful, knowledgeable few. The monster is "the embodiment of an ideal state of being [and] serves as a nostalgic frame of reference to an earlier day of innocence." However, the manipulation of those people who exist in every technological society will eventually result in confrontation and this face to face meeting will be disastrous.

> The oppressor and the oppressed, the definer and the defined, must sometimes face each other. One-dimensionality means they can do so as human beings.

Crafts takes what seems to be the classic stand in the evaluation of speculative fiction and of *Frankenstein:* they can only be judged pessimistic in outlook. The combatants in this scientific/humanitarian war will necessarily "kill each other," a fact which he concludes "so far . . . seems terribly accurate." Science offers no hope, only death for both man and his creations. He consequently views Victor as a "latter-day Faust" whose "professed project of domination of nature" will inevitably lead to disastrous consequences.

P. D. Fleck's article is an important contribution to the criticism on *Frankenstein*.[36] He makes a lucid and determined effort to analyze the meaning of the novel and, to my mind, is one of the most successful. He seeks to establish the point that "Mary's belated contribution to the discussions of idealism which took place in 1816, were made through her revisions of the poems and comments she attached to the edition of Shelley's collected works." Fleck sets forth the literary analogues of *Frankenstein* that may have contributed to the creation of the story. He points out that the novel had its inception in the "Shelley-Byron menage" of 1816 as they "sat around the fire reading short stories." However, he is quick to add that the care Mary extended to the writing of this book was immense and not the quickly churned out product that some critics have pictured.

> She spent more time writing *Frankenstein* than Shelley did on any of his works, and the revisions of certain parts of the manuscript speak loudly of the difficulties she faced.

Fleck also believes that Mary owed more of the story to Polidori than she credits and cites a Polidori journal entry of a conversation with Shelley at which Mary was present, during which the "possibility of creating life" was discussed. After a discussion of Victor's motives, Fleck discusses several literary analogues to *Frankenstein*.

He sees in Aeschylus's *Prometheus Bound* an implicit assumption that "man is made to submit to powers greater than himself," and that the reader is meant to feel this in the failure of Victor to control his android. William Backford's *Vathek* is another analogue to *Frankenstein* in that it is about "an insolent desire to penetrate the secrets of heaven." Vathek's fate is similar to Victor's.

> Such was and such should be the punishment of unbridled passions and atrocious deeds; such will be the guerdon of blind curiosity which desires to penetrate beyond the bounds which the Creator has placed to human knowledge, of ambition which, wishing to acquire sciences reserved for purer intelligences, gains only an insensate pride, and does not perceive that the lot of man is to be humble and ignorant.[37]

Goethe's *Sorrows of Werther* contains nearly the same echo in the hero's "inordinate desire . . . for better humanity." Mary and her husband read *Werther* in 1815 and Fleck sees it as a possible source of Victor's attitude. Fleck also shows how Godwin's *St. Leon* and *Caleb Williams* exhibit the same thirst for knowledge seen in Victor to an inordinate degree. St.

Leon entertains a nearly fanatical passion for the philosopher's stone and it is this zeal that destroys him. Caleb Williams's "offense" was "merely a mistaken thirst for knowledge." *Childe Harold* also offers a large number of similarities upon which Mary might have drawn her character Victor, but it is to Shelley's "Alastor" that the strongest tie can be seen. Victor and the narrator of this poem both have a "desire for knowledge that is unsatisfied"; they are both men who desire "to know the secret principles of life."

> . . . I have watched
> Thy shadow, and the darkness of thy steps,
> And my heart ever gazes on the depth
> Of thy deep mysteries.[38]

Like Victor, the hero of Shelley's poem has had close association with the dead and the things of the dead. A haunter of the charnel house and an observer of coffins,

> . . . I have made my bed
> In charnels and on coffins, where black death
> Keeps record of the trophies won from thee,
> Hoping to still these abstinate questionings
> Of thee and thine, by forcing some lone ghost
> Thy messenger, to render up the tale
> Of what we are.

There follows a lengthy comparison of the two works, but the emphasis is on the way in which knowledge is a destroyer of man, not a savior. Fleck arrives at his conclusions easily:

> Mary leaves the hard but, as far as she is concerned, unquestionable moral. There is a sense of tragedy but there is also the hope of consolation and it lies in human society. It lies in learning the lesson . . . Mary says in effect, that one must seek tranquility and moderation.

E. Nageswara Rao is the only critic who discusses the actual structure of the novel.[39] He sees *Frankenstein* as a "Chinese-box structure" of three concentric circles. Rao believes that the "innermost circle" can be made to represent "the Monster and his horrors." On the other hand the "outermost" of the circles represents reality. He regards Frankenstein, Walton, and the artificial man as different parts of the same personality. He devotes his discussion to the structure of the novel and the consequences it has for the working out of the character development.

Dr. Masao Miyoshi discusses the "Faustian thirst for knowledge" so often associated with Victor and his ultimate punishment.⁴⁰ He believes the novel is the usual Gothic tale filled with "the terror and brutality; the lightening on the bones; [etc.]." He does observe that the Gothic supernaturalism has been converted to a kind of scientism that retains all the flavor of the Gothic atmosphere. "If scientific man is a kind of God," Miyoshi maintains, "his scientific method becomes a new kind of supernaturalism." He makes a valid comment on the book but does not have the space in his work to develop this idea at greater length. This scientism will be examined later in this study.

Milton Mays sees *Frankenstein* as a "very bookish book."⁴¹ Although he too feels it is "permeated with literary allusions, quotations, references, and parallels," he is drawn most strongly to the Faust myth and Milton's *Paradise Lost*. Mays discerns two themes in *Frankenstein*. First there is an "outer one" in which he sees Victor as a "chastened Faust." This outer theme also examines the story of the android himself, "the victim of universal injustice—from man and from his 'God' Frankenstein. . . ." But there is also an "inner theme" which Mays describes as a "black theodicy" in which the android is seen as a kind of Romantic rebel, typical of its kind and being in its full composition a collection of "Romantic archetypes." The monster also stands as a symbol for the heroic outcast and as such must inevitably be compared to Adam and Satan, whom the android frequently alludes to in his narrative. But there is a most important difference:

> The significant feature of contrast between Milton's Satan, who, orthodoxly understood, does his part in justifying God's ways to man, and Mary Shelley's monster, is that Satan's misery springs from his crime, the Monster's crime from his misery.

Mays considers the monster's life style to be a product of its rejection by men and his creator. Therefore, the monster sets about systematically to destroy all people who are connected to Frankenstein himself. Mays comes to the conclusion that the world Mary Shelley depicts is "a dark one" in which "fundamental injustice prevails among men."

Another provocative article about *Frankenstein* is that of Sylva Norman.⁴² She admits that *Frankenstein* is a novel of speculative fiction, but is scornful of the result. She obviously does not like speculative fiction as a genre and her attitude shows clearly in a series of heavily biased statements. For instance, she does not like to consider seriously Mary's depiction of Victor piecing the monster's body together. Norman finds it unthinkable that sections of different human bodies could be brought together into a coherent whole. As a result, Norman is unable to bring about the willing suspension of disbelief necessary to see Victor and his project as experimental science. For her it is pure horror and nonsense. Norman is more comfortable discussing Mary's moral preoccupations, but, again, the book is marred further for her when Mary intersperses scientific experiment with "tales of family origins and misfortunes." In her views Norman is traditional, perpetuating the judgments of the *Quarterly Review*.

M. K. Joseph's introduction to the standard Oxford edition of *Frankenstein* surveys the main ideas in a brief but complete essay.[43] He points to all the critical ideas (such as the Promethean background, the moral implications of the work, etc.) but he says nothing about the scientific possibilities that the novel suggests. Mr. Joseph's essay is a concise survey of the standard critical positions.

One of the most perceptive and interesting statements about *Frankenstein* was made in 1972 by Robert Kiely.[44] Approaching the novel from a romantic consideration, he includes the novel as one of several he believes fall into the characteristic pattern of the romantic novel, i.e., a reaction against the straightforward common sense of the mainstream tradition.

He analyzes the major themes and motifs in *Frankenstein* as he sees them, such as "superiority through suffering" and the exaltation of the "hero without reproach [Victor]." One of his most important contributions to the critical tradition is a lengthy discussion of how Mary used Victor to treat "the material consequences of his theoretical projects." He notes that in so doing, Mary's work resembles speculative fiction as we know it and that consideration of the book must take this into account. On the whole, this review gives one of the best and coolest assessments I have read, criticizing with candor and fairness both the novel as a work of art and Mary as the writer of a valuable piece of fiction.

Aija Ozolins in an unpublished dissertation attempts "to undertake to present a balanced and unified view of Mary as a novelist."[45] She takes as truth Mary's relation of the circumstances of the novel's inception as a dream product, and devotes all of her commentary to showing how this works out in the mythic elements of the story. Since her main thesis is to show similarities and patterns among six novels of Mary Shelley, she spends little time on each one, choosing only those aspects of the novel as fit her pattern to comment upon. She does allude to the scientific aspects of *Frankenstein;* its relationship to Locke and scientists such as Trembley and Needham. She discusses the science of the book, but her thesis does not allow her time to go into great detail about the relationship between the new science and the novel.

The latest biography of Mary Shelley by Noel Gerson is entitled *Daughter of Earth and Water* and has little to add to the critical tradition.[46] He contents himself with a simple resumé of the facts of the origin of the novel, makes a few remarks about its Gothic character, and calls attention to the standard ideas about the book. His main judgment is this:

> The novel is regarded as a story to be enjoyed, perhaps a curiosity. The scholar does not classify it as literature, in part because Mary told her story in the convoluted form popular in her day, and partly because her language was graceless and her characterizations lacked subtlety.

Martin Tropp, in an unpublished dissertation entitled "Mary Shelley's Monster: A Study of *Frankenstein*," attempts to show how the "social, biographical, moral and psychological levels intertwine" in *Frankenstein* to present one moral, "the dangers of isolation."[47] Tropp sees the novel as a moral fable. For Tropp Mary's message is simply that "science threatens mankind." His position is not new but represents a synthesis of the views taken by a great many critics. He believes his investigation is "the first extended study" of the novel. He does not appear to be aware of Small's book-length investigation of the mythic elements of *Frankenstein* nor does he mention Rieger or Fleck and the work they have done on the backgrounds of the novel. His viewpoint is the complete opposite of mine and indicates the diversity of views that the novel generates. A comparison of Mary's views represented by this statement, with those of Kiely shows well how wildly the critics differ in their estimate of the book as a novel and as a piece of writing.

Patrick J. Callahan's article "*Frankenstein*, Bacon, and the Two Truths," along with Pollin examines the scientific background of Mary's novel.[48] Callahan concerns himself with the way in which *Frankenstein* seems to be a "satire on the deficiencies of science," and the relationship science has to the "ancient pseudo-scientist . . . Cornelius Agrippa and Paracelsus." He amplifies this statement as follows:

> Through an exploration of her [Mary's] use of allusion to the occultist, it is possible to qualify many of her attitudes toward the "new science" of her time, and such an investigation may thus serve to temper the simplistic truism that she was "against empirical science as forbidden knowledge."

As a consequence, Callahan believes that Mary was deliberately satirizing "an implicit philosophy of science," a philosophy he terms "Baconian optimism." He is disturbed that the critics who "take endless interest in the Miltonic or Promethean echoes of Frankenstein's speeches" have never taken it upon themselves to "stress" that "Frankenstein is an empirical scientist, with all the progressivist prejudices of the Enlightenment blatantly obvious in his narrative." Although he does no more than suggest this Baconian alignment, the narrow space of his article not permitting more, he does satisfactorily point out the relationship. The critics have thus far only been interested in "stressing the old" and, in so doing, "neglected the new." One of the most interesting points in Callahan's article is his presentation of Victor's speech followed by a totally new critical comment about the relationship of Victor to the new science.

> The materials at present within my command hardly appeared adequate to so arduous an undertaking; but I doubted not that I should ultimately succeed. . . . When I considered the science and mechanics, I was encouraged to hope my present attempt would at least lay the foundations of future success.[49]

It is in such lines as these that Callahan sees Victor echo

> Bacon's belief that scientific investigation will render nature's secrets open to man's control as well as Bacon's faith that no natural mystery, despite momentary setbacks is beyond the systematic application of the empirical method.

For the first time in the critical history of *Frankenstein* a comment that fully takes into consideration the scientific aspects of the novel has been made. Its deepest fault lies in its brevity. It only hints about the layers of science that lie beneath the surface. Some commentators have been disturbed that because Mary did not reveal the actual method by which Victor conferred life upon his creation she committed a serious error. However there are few, if any, novels of speculative fiction that pretend seriously to explain in detail the scientific processes, techniques, or theories by which their heroes succeed. The processes producing the invention or technological advancement are carefully shrouded in mystery. In concealing the secret of the spark of life, Mary anticipates the method of the speculative fiction story in general: like all good speculative fiction writers she bases her product on the extrapolation of known processes, theorizing that this process will somehow be successful even if the steps to that end are not yet known. All of Victor's scientific studies can be traced in eighteenth-century science. There is not a statement made by Mary that does not have at least one, sometimes dozens, of echoes in the scientific literature of her age.

Another significant addition to the criticism that views *Frankenstein* as a novel of speculative fiction is the initial chapter of Brian Aldiss's study of speculative fiction. In his lengthy book, *The Billion Year Spree,* the entire first chapter is devoted to Mary Shelley.[50] It deals with *Frankenstein,* the scientific aspects of the eighteenth century, and their possible effect on Mary's novel.

Aldiss examines *Frankenstein* as a serious candidate for the title of the first speculative fiction novel. He calls attention to the connection the novel has with Darwin's *Zoonomia*. Aldiss also quotes several lines from Darwin's *The Temple of Nature* that prophesy such things as the automobile and the nuclear submarine. As a result of this line of thought, Aldiss believes Darwin qualifies as a "part-time science-fiction writer." Most of the chapter is devoted to a recapitulation of the plot and the mythic qualities of *Frankenstein*. Aldiss does say that "as a science fiction morality" the story is "no less powerful today than when it was written surrounded as we are with so many fiends of our own designing." Nothing new is thought out. The important factor is the recognition given to the novel as something more than a storehouse of Miltonic analogues and Promethean echoes; it becomes recognized as a novel that belongs without question in the genre of speculation and of speculative fiction, placed there by a well-known and prolific writer of speculative fiction.

Although Christopher Small is not a literary critic, he has written the first full length study of the novel.[51] His book displays a broad awareness of a variety of subjects related to the Romantic Movement in general and Mary Shelley in particular. The book itself announces it will "trace the myth" and leans heavily upon a variety of secondary sources for its conclusions, rather than drawing conclusions from original research.

The opening chapters recount the early life of Mary Shelley and her training by Godwin. Small is most concerned, however, with the tale as a myth. "Mythology," he observes, "is a metaphorical thinking in which the metaphor assumes independent and continuing existence." Mythology is strongly dependent upon metaphor to know existence and, as Small expresses it, "is usually thought of as a product of individual fancy or conceit, and the part only from many of which a larger whole, myth or work of art, is constructed." But, he believes, there are metaphors and then there are metaphors. The common kind one quickly realizes is used only as a fleeting basis of comparison, pleasant as we read it, but not pervasive. There is another kind of metaphor which "is itself a work of art," borrowing its being from both the known and the unknown to make a "third, independent and new." Such a metaphor is *Frankenstein*, as it "conveys within it powerful and manifold meanings" that take on a kind of life of their own, allowing us to see an increasing number of relationships suggested and, with the passing of time, are seen to be increasingly applicable. Of this phenomenon Small comments:

> At these times, one may say, a metaphor turns up new or significantly modified, a sport or mutation in this analogue of organic evolution. Like such it may die out quickly or it may permanently influence the development of myth, and through it the growth from individual genesis to generalized existence can be studied and, perhaps, partially understood. Such a natural history of metaphor is exemplified in *Frankenstein*.

The rest of the chapter is a full-scale study of the Frankenstein myth as it made its way to public notice through contemporary reviews, the drama, and the cinema. But at the end of the chapter, Small announces his real purpose for writing this book. He will:

> examine the "peculiar" circumstances that awakened her [Mary's] thoughts, and to guess at some of the components of the thoughts themselves, as the first objects of inquiry. They can be arranged under three heads. First there are the actual circumstances of the author at the time, well-known and attested. Secondly, the direct influence, both literary and personal that may be inferred from the book itself and from what is known of Mary Shelley's reading of her character, and the character of those intimately associated with her. Thirdly, there are the more remote or indirect forces brought to bear upon the book, social and historical, including its own distinct effects.

In working out this methodology few of the remarks made by Small are original. Most have appeared elsewhere as a reading of the existing criticism and biographical material will reveal. It is little more than a compilation of knowledge already known, gathered under one title. He is most concerned with the relationship of *Frankenstein* to the myth of Prometheus and spends a great deal of time showing the pertinent associations with the Promethean myth and the way it has been rehandled by Mary. He also takes a great deal of time along the way to indicate that for him the book is less reliant upon scientific reading than it is on mythic sources, and is chiefly concerned with the moral responsibilities of man as they are often negated by man himself. He believes that *Frankenstein* shows us the moral reprehensibility of modern man as he tries to be of use to mankind and fails in the attempt, largely through an abuse of knowledge. Like Kingsley Amis's view of speculative fiction in his *New Maps of Hell*, Small believes that speculative fiction adopts a strongly pessimistic tone in which it disparages man's ability ever to truly master science. Rather, science will master man and, concomitant with this belief, *Frankenstein* serves as a prime example. For Small, speculative fiction represents a "typical mode" in the dispensing of this pessimism.

> This seems to be that kind of obsessional fantasy which at once partially quietens and feeds on underlying fear, and which becomes, in the absence of insight, progressively more acute. The mechanical futures envisaged in these fantasies are nearly always terrible, the very act of imagining them leads logically to the attempt to imagine a world without men.

Small spends a great deal of time developing the idea that speculative fiction serves in the role of a prophet of doom, foreseeing a universe in which machines do away with men. "There is no *reason* why the machine, which is a reasonable device," Small observes, "should not—

having thoroughly subdued man and assumed control over his life—in due course abolish him."

William A. Walling's critical view of *Frankenstein* is one of the most searching and successful general statements about the novel in modern criticism.[52] The chapter on *Frankenstein,* part of a book on Mary Shelley and her fiction, offers a composite statement about the novel but at the same time offers several new comments.

Walling largely ignores the scientific issues, preferring to restate the facts of the novel's origin, the history of its composition, its publication and initial reception, the broad structure of the novel, the dual role of Frankenstein and the Godwinian influence. Most of what he says has been stated by other critics so there is no point in repeating it. This, of course, is exactly what the book is intended to do.

Any student of *Frankenstein* who desires a rapid survey of the outstanding critical views of the novel will find this work indispensable. Walling correctly points out that the novel shows Frankenstein as a "radically divided Prometheus who is unable . . . to reconcile man's hopeless conflict between his emotional nature and his intellectual ambitions." This point has often been missed by commentators and, in my view, it is essential to an understanding of the novel. Walling sees Frankenstein as a man whose "true failure" is not that his artificial man has run amok, but that it has gone mad from the "inadequacy of [Frankenstein's] love."

The last piece of serious criticism I have inspected is once again by James Rieger.[53] The article is his introduction to the new edition of *Frankenstein* already alluded to. As with all introductions to the novel, he surveys existing opinions, but the most interesting statement concerns the science in the book, which he finds is very unscientific. "Frankenstein's chemistry is switched-on magic, souped-up alchemy, the electrification of Agrippa and Paracelsus."[54] I will challenge this statement because Mary was more in command of her creative processes and more knowledgeable about science than that. She does not "skip the science" as Rieger seems to believe.[55] However, the introduction is valuable because it is written by a man who has investigated the work well and is totally familiar with its background. Therefore his opinions are not to be lightly dismissed, and it must be noted that he does a fine job of summarizing many key critical ideas about the novel. He is, however, much more interested in the symbolic and allegorical message of *Frankenstein* and remains to a degree embarrassed that it might be classified as speculative fiction.

Radu Florescu has contributed the second full-length study of *Frankenstein*.[56] As a summer citizen of Geneva, he is familiar with the physical aspects of Swiss geography and has related them to the specific places visited by Mary Shelley. The work is not meant to be a scholarly treatise (as the rather vulgar title indicates), but is, rather, a semi-popular rehearsal of the biography of Mary Shelley and its relationship to the physical landscape of Switzerland. The heart of Florescu's book is the attempt to account for the origin of the name Frankenstein. He shows that Mary and Percy Shelley passed very close to the vicinity of the castle of the Barons Frankenstein and that they could (although no mention is made of the fact in extant diaries or journals) have visited it. He also brings to the reader's attention the fact that the castle passed into the hands of an alchemist named Konrad Dippel who, legend has it, attempted to learn the secret of life and experimented with the elixir of life and the philosopher's stone. The book is a survey similar to Walling's but immeasurably inferior to it. He covers much territory but he unfortunately bases much of his argument on hearsay and gossip, extant stories, and interested people. His book is to be taken into account with the utmost care.

Such, then, is the long critical tradition surrounding Mary Shelley's greatest novel. The traditional critics see a strong parallel between Frankenstein and Shelley, or between Mary Shelley's inner experiences and understanding with her outer relationships with her husband or life in general. Science is seen as far-reaching in its effects but sadly in need of enormous control, a situation the majority of commentators believe Mary was illustrating.

In other words, the roots of rationalism lead to the greatest mistakes and the novel presents a fable for man, a prophetic lesson, which we dare not miss. In addition, the literary antecedents of *Frankenstein* are closely examined and exhaustively traced. Most of the major echoes and analogues are reviewed by Pollin, Rieger, Fleck, and Mays who all, while differing in small respects, view the book as a tissue of literary allusions which in one way or another contribute to the genesis of the novel. None of them attempts to examine the Paracelsian canon for analogues or to study Erasmus Darwin to determine how much Mary owes to him in the formulation of her scientific insights. For the question must be asked: How much of her idea did she owe to scientific sources and in what way did she view the older scientists? Many of Victor's scientific studies and attitudes can be traced in eighteenth-century science. Until now, except for Pollin and Callahan, literary critics have not taken sufficient notice of the scientific background of Mary's age or read much in the scientific affairs of her time.

3

The Problem of the Text

The study of the scientific backgrounds of *Frankenstein* is complicated by the evolution of the novel itself from the manuscript begun in 1816 to the last, official, printed version of 1831. These fifteen years saw the novel shaped by both Mary and Percy Shelley. The modern reader is accustomed to a text of *Frankenstein* based on the 1831 edition, but this does not faithfully represent the material present in Mary's mind when she began the book in 1816. There are, then, several problems that must be considered when selecting a proper text for a study of this kind.

The manuscript survives in two parts and is preserved in the so-called Abinger collection now in the custody of the Bodleian Library.[1] These portions are nearly complete. Missing are Walton's letters and about the last one-sixth of the novel. The rest is intact. The manuscript was written on large, blank, folio paper measuring 11½ by 17 inches. Many of these pages are ruled with a vertical line that forms a three-inch margin on the left side of the page. It is in this margin that the emendations, many ascribed to Shelley, are written.

I was able to examine the manuscript from a microfilm copy in the possession of Duke University. The first part of the novel is found on reel 6 together with letters of Mary Shelley and Claire Clairmont, as well as part of John Gisbourne's *Journal*. This portion of the manuscript is fairly consecutive. If this is the working manuscript, which shows the daily growth of the novel, and not simply a fair copy, it indicates that Mary wrote her book steadily, with a clear conception of the story line. Few paragraphs are deleted and few individual words are crossed out.

The other portion of the manuscript is found on reel 11. This part also is written on the same, large, folio paper, but the chapters are in confusion. Not only are they not consecutive, but unused portions of paper at the end of chapters are used to record later sections of the novel without regard for order. It is not possible to follow the story line from this section of the manuscript although the pages show that Mary worked steadily and without hesitation here as well.

In both portions of the manuscript there are relatively few marginal notations. These are, without exception, emendations of sentence structure or additions to the text. There are no places where the author has placed data on the origin of her ideas for the story nor where the marginal note questions an idea expressed in the text. There are, however, several places where the text differs from the published version of 1818 and the deleted material shows some interesting highlights of Mary's thoughts about the background of the novel and sheds some light on her knowledge at the time of composition.

Several conclusions may be drawn from the state of the manuscript. The fact that there is little hesitancy in the narrative flow suggests that Mary was already familiar with the scientific elements she used. It further suggests that she knew more about scientific matters and was more interested in these matters than she is generally given credit for. It also suggests that the novel, except for very small editorial changes, was Mary's creative product and not Shelley's.

The novel was published anonymously in March 1818 by Lackington, Hughes, Harding, Mayor, and Jones of Finsbury Square, London. This version has been reprinted by James Rieger and presents the book as it was initially conceived by Mary.[2] It is this version that I will use as the basis for my quotations and investigation. Rieger's work is valuable because in appendix B of his book a collation of the text of 1818 and the text of 1831 is provided. This new material may not all be Mary's work. It is suspected that Shelley had a strong hand in this last revision.

It should be noted that while these additions do change the book in its shape to a degree, they do not substantially alter its scientific tone nor do they add a great deal of new material as some critics have asserted. In fact, the changes often only amplify the material that was present in the 1818 version.

The second edition published in 1823 was a two-volume, page by page copy of the 1818 edition. No changes were made. Also in 1823, Mary presented to her friend Mrs. Thomas a copy of *Frankenstein* with autograph corrections. These corrections are few, concerning themselves with stylistic matters only. They do not alter the intellectual content of the book in any way. These variants were not used for the 1831 edition and until Rieger's edition of *Frankenstein* were unknown except to specialists.

It is the 1831 version, with its long, new introduction by Mary and the addition of much new material, with which the modern reader is most familiar.[3] Although most publishers of *Frankenstein* do not pinpoint the origin of their texts, the dozens of editions that exist today are copies of the one-volume text published in 1831 by Henry Colburn and Richard

Bentley. The novel was listed as number nine in their series of "Standard Novels."

Despite the completeness and the ubiquitousness of this edition of *Frankenstein,* Rieger's edition has been used for citations of the text. It shows the original intent of the authoress and permits correlation with the variant readings as they later appeared in 1831. In addition, it includes the autograph revisions appearing in Mrs. Thomas's novel. Through the 1818 text a more accurate picture of the novel may be drawn as it retains Mary Shelley's original concept of the novel with greater fidelity.

4

The Literature on Artificial Humans Prior to 1818

An examination of the scientific backgrounds of Mary Shelley's *Frankenstein* must of necessity examine the artificial man as a product of a scientific experiment. This is necessary because Victor Frankenstein is presented as an advocate of the new science and the humanoid he constructs is developed theoretically and actually on methods derived from the new science. All of the critical literature has ignored this point of view. The lack of discussion of Shelley's artificial man as a scientific product can be ascribed to the fact that the critics have normally focused their attention on the novel as a moral fable. In this context the artificial human is regarded as an agent of evil, the symbol of powerful, new, unleashed forces which man is not yet able to control.

Therefore, this chapter will offer an alternative reading in which the artificial man presented in the novel will be regarded solely as a product of the inquiries resulting from the applied methods of the new science. The destructive nature of the Being will be ignored in order to focus on the artificial man itself: its exterior physical appearance; its interior construction; the method of its animation; its emotional nature; and its relationship to other artificial men present in literature prior to 1818.

The physical body of Mary Shelley's artificial man has excited the most attention. But the application of various names such as "monster," "spectre," "fiend," "filthy daemon," etc., have all tended to obscure its physical outlines. To be sure, its grotesque face and great height—both factors that are used in the novel to create a feeling of horror and an atmosphere of terror—prevent the Being from being viewed with scientific detachment. But it must be borne in mind that Victor Frankenstein's judgment when he assesses this physical appearance for the reader is not reliable. He is, as he himself admits, suffering from a general nervous collapse, completely precipitated by his success in animating his humanoid. He has suffered from "days and nights of incredible fatigue," during which his "cheek had grown pale with study" and his "person emaciated with confinement."[1] He tells us that he was "oppressed by a slow fever" and "became nervous to a most painful degree."[2] Ultimately he becomes "as timid as a love-sick girl."[3] Victor, alone and assailed by anxiety, is in no condition to accept ultimate success nor to face a huge and unknown artificial man. Such a state of mind renders him unfit to pass any judgments and this state of mind is compounded by the Being's murder of Victor's family.

The novel, however, provides another personality who can give a much more sane evaluation of this large humanoid. Robert Walton is also a scientist, and, it must not be forgotten, through him the story is transmitted to his sister Mrs. Saville. Walton, although without formal scientific training, has imbibed the scientific attitude of the new science, particularly skepticism and personal observation. He has come to the Arctic region where the book opens in order to prove to himself and to the world whether the stories, myths, and legends that had long been accepted as fact about this place were, in fact, true. He briefly summarizes some of these legends in his letter to his sister of December 11.[4]

> There snow and frost are banished; and sailing over a calm sea, we may be wafted to a land hitherto undiscovered on the habitable globe. Its productions and features may be without example . . . What may not be expected in a country [of eternal light?] . . . I may there discover the wondrous power which attracts the needle; and may regulate a thousand celestial observations—that require only this voyage to render their seeming eccentricities consistent forever.[5]

Walton is well versed on the legends of the Arctic. Realizing that they may well be fables, he is excited about the truth of the discoveries that he may make. Notice the clear skepticism in Walton's thought indicated by the use of "may." He has not closed his mind to the possibility that the error of former authorities may lead to direct, fresh observation. It is through his eyes that the reader first sees the artificial man. Although he calls this sight a "strange . . . accident" and remarks further that "this appearance excited our unqualified wonder," the words he uses to describe the Being are sober and of a scientific rather than sensational cast.[6]

> About two o'clock the mist cleared away, and we beheld, stretched out in every direction, vast and irregular [mountains &] plains of ice, which seemed to have no end. Some of my comrades groaned, and my own mind began to grow watchful with anxious thoughts, when a strange sight suddenly attracted our attention, and diverted our solicitude from our own situation. We perceived a low carriage, fixed on a sledge and drawn by dogs . . . a being which had the shape of a man, but apparently of gigantic stature, sat in the sledge, and guided the dogs.[7]

The reader's first glimpse of the artificial man is presented without hysteria. We merely see a gigantic human sitting in a sledge. But cool evaluation at a distance is one thing; a face to face meeting with a being that has frightened into madness every human it has met is quite another.

Walton's scientific detachment does not fail him when he personally faces the Being at the end of the novel after his mind has had a chance to be set on edge by the harrowing language Victor uses to tell Walton his story.[8] Walton does not run away and observes the creature at close range carefully. He relates that he sees "a form."[9] Although he "cannot find words to describe" the form of the Being, he does not resort to hysterical or vicious language. Once again the creature is "gigantic in stature" and its "proportions" are "uncouth and distorted." Beyond this, all he chooses to record is that the Being has a "vast hand," the skin of which was "in colour and texture like that of a mummy." The face was "concealed by long locks of ragged hair." There is, therefore, a definite precedent for careful observation, permitting us to view the artificial man with eyes unfilled with Gothic horror.

For a more complete description of the artificial man we are unfortunately forced to use Victor's own observations. However, through the aura of nightmare, it is possible to see a number of features clearly enabling us to form a slightly clearer view of it. We are told by Victor that he planned the giant size of the humanoid deliberately for a practical reason. He could not, he discovered, make the body smaller because the "minuteness of the parts" of a normal sized human were "a great hindrance to my speed."[10] He resolved "to make the being of a gigantic stature; that is to say, about eight feet in height, and proportionably large." But what precisely did it look like when it was finished?

Mary did not give us an exact description and if the working manuscript of the novel we have is an accurate guide, there are no cancelled passages that elaborate on the features of the artificial man. From the hints left here and there we know that the skin was "shrivelled," "yellow," and had "the texture of that of a mummy."[11] This skin "scarcely covered" the "muscles and arteries" beneath. Evidently it had been pieced together and stretched tight, but there must have been gaps at the seams. The head is covered by black hair which Victor describes as being "lustrous" and "flowing."

The eyes of the artificial man were "watery," set in "dun white sockets," and are first described as "dull yellow." The only other exterior features described are the lips which were "straight," "black," and "thin" behind which could be seen teeth of "pearly whiteness." All other descriptions of the exterior form of the artificial man are couched in expressions of horror. Even the monster's view of itself in a pool does not try to create an exact, realistic portrait.[12]

Beneath this unusual surface we are able to glimpse an anatomical mechanism that is similar to the human body. We know that the parts for this body came from three places: (1) the charnel house, (2) the slaughter pen, and (3) the dissection room. Victor had evidently planned in minute detail the body of the artificial man because he knew what parts he needed in advance. He tells us that they were selected, arranged, and organized before he began the complex task of assembling the body of the humanoid, a task which took him "months."[13]

The assembly of these parts is extremely difficult. Despite the unusual knowledge of anatomy Victor is pictured as possessing, his labor to bring together these disparate parts into a coherent whole undermines his physical well-being and destroys his analytical judgment. Victor finally succeeds in fitting the parts together, but he fails to produce a handsome exterior. I believe that under ordinary circumstances and under his usually controlled state of mind he would have recognized that he had produced a working prototype which required refinement. As it was, he only saw that as a sculptor of flesh he had not lived up to his own expectations. His weakened mind sickened and recoiled when he saw the actual features of his artificial man and as a result he abandoned it at birth. Be that as it may, he was able to successfully join the parts to prepare it for the final stage of the experiment: animation. Like the features of the artificial man, Mary Shelley provides only the most sketchy details about the process that animated Victor's cybernetic robot. His knowledge of natural philosophy transcends that of his teachers and enters new, untrodden fields of experiment. We are given the picture of a man who has learned all that his school at Ingolstadt can teach regarding natural philosophy. Victor tells us that "when I had arrived at this point, and had become as well acquainted with the theory and practice of natural philosophy as depended on the lessons of any of the professors at Ingolstadt, my residence there being no longer conducive to my improvements, I thought of returning to my native town, when an incident happened that protracted my stay."[14]

This incident was directly concerned with "one of the phaenomena which had particularly attracted" him, i.e., the principle of life. He launches himself into a course of study and experiment very much outside the normal inquiry of the university. His study is so successful that "after days and nights of incredible labor and fatigue, I succeeded in discovering the cause and generation of life."[15] And not only is he able to understand the secret, he himself becomes "capable of bestowing animation upon lifeless matter." How such an effect is transmitted there are few hints.

We know that its discovery was in "stages" that were "distinct and probable," and that its production had to be effected by means of scientific instruments. We also know that the spark of life must be transferred from a living animal to a dead one. Victor speaks of torturing "the living animal to animate the lifeless clay."[16] It may be connected to the experiments with electricity on living and dead animals that one finds so commonly in the writings of Galvani, Priestley, Volta, and others.[17]

However, whatever the exact method used to impart life to the eight-foot corpse lying on the floor in Victor's attic rooms, the fact remains that it *is* imparted. On the evening when Victor is successful, he is pictured as gathering "the instruments of life" around him.[18] These instruments are about to infuse "a spark of being into the lifeless thing" that "lay at [his] feet." The process is not described and of course cannot be. Mary Shelley, like all writers of speculative fiction, must leave that last step to the imaginations of the readers. This is the unknown quantity that separates fact from fiction and Mary does not know the secret she ascribes to Victor any more than we do. She does, however, imagine the process of animation as a tedious one and not particularly spectacular to watch. When, after patient effort (the candle he had lit at the beginning of this final evening in his laboratory had nearly burned out) he is successful, the description of the Being coming to life is almost prosaic. The eye of the great Being opens; it breathes "hard," and "a convulsive motion agitated its limbs."[19] Thus the springs of life begin to run in the artificial man.

Mary Shelley has thus accounted for several aspects of the artificial man. She has given it interior parts and exterior shape, and discussed the manner of animation. Now she provides us with a close look at its interior life. The reader is very quickly made aware that the Being is not merely gigantic in size. Its emotional states and mode of life are equally gigantic.

It is the complexity of this inner life, and the psychological states, that raises Mary Shelley's artificial man far above any similar human simulacrum postulated prior to 1818—except the statue in Condillac's *Treatise on the Sensations*. Mary takes great care to present this aspect of the artificial man in its own words, almost as though Condillac's statue had come to life and could speak to us. But she elects to present the large mass of detail and anecdote exemplifying the sensationalist psychology of Condillac against an outline of ideas found in David Hartley's *Observations on Man, His Frame, His Duty, and His Expectations*.[20] This factor alone immediately throws the novel into a scientifically based category.

There is no direct evidence from the reading lists Mary gave in her journal, or those subsequently deduced by her biographers, that she knew about Hartley. We do know that Shelley in 1812 bought a copy of this book and it is assumed he read it.[21] Perhaps in the long conversations at the Villa Diodati between Shelley and Byron, Hartley's observations were mentioned; and Mary, silently participating, learned Hartley's basic beliefs and their connection with Condillac. The intellectual progress of the artificial man parallels very closely the ideas in Hartley's *Observations*, and it is more than likely that this book served as a strong theoretical foundation upon which to build ideas of the interior awakening of the artificial man.

Part I of Hartley's work proceeds immediately to definitions. He divides the being of man into two parts—body and mind—both of which are interrelated. His use of mind negates a belief in the soul and adopts the philosophy of materialism about which W. C. Dampier observed that "thought and consciousness are but by-products of matter, and that there is nothing real underlying it or existing beyond it."[22] This would account for the fact that the artificial man has no memory of a past life and is a unique personality. The materialism fostered by the new science and which caused deeply religious men such as Hartley to have intellectual problems with their line of thinking becomes strongly evident early in the novel.

Presumably the brain of the artificial man was one selected from those available in the dissecting room or the slaughter house. The size of the Being argues that its brain is a composite of organic tissue because the bulk of the average human brain would not by itself fill the cranial space of the artificial man's huge head (assuming all its parts were, as Victor asserts, like its limbs, "in proportion").[23] This combination would give rise to a new personality which would have no memory of a former life. This is entirely consistent with the views of empirical materialism which assumed that the body was not operated by an invisible anima but was, rather, animated through the strict law of necessity resulting from an interaction of the body parts.[24]

Hartley is an empirical materialist because he makes it clear in Part I that ideas are the result of sensations alone. He states that "internal feelings of the mind, which arise from the impressions made by external objects upon the several parts of our bodies" are called "sensations."[25] "Ideas" are "all the other internal feelings." Ideas of sensation give rise to intellectual ideas. The former "are the elements of which all the rest are compounded."

Sensations are categorized into two parts: (1) pleasures and (2) pains. These he arranges into seven general classes: (1) sensations, (2) imagination, (3) ambition, (4) self-interest, (5) sympathy, (6) theopathy, (7) the moral sense. The Being's experiences can be shown as falling into these categories, and in the order they are presented by Hartley.

We are given an extensive and detailed account of the Being's early experiences with reality. This information, given autobiographically, begins with the Being's earliest memories and ends with the discovery of its origin provided by the laboratory notes of Victor Frankenstein, discovered in the pocket of the dressing gown it put on when it fled from the place of its birth. The first thing that enters the Being's awareness is sensation. "A strange multiplicity of sensations seized me, and I saw, heard, and smelt, at the same time; and it was indeed, a long time before I learned to distinguish between the operations of my various senses."[26] These sensations are described in considerable detail covering several pages of explanation.

Out of this early experience, the Being emerges as a living creature to distinguish the different parts of its environment. "My sensations had," it tells Victor, "by this time, become distinct, and my mind received every day additional ideas. My eyes became accustomed to the light, and to perceive objects in their right forms; I distinguished the insect from the herb, and, by degrees, one herb from another."[27]

This impact of physical sensation gives rise to Hartley's second category, imagination. The imagination of the artificial being is stimulated in a variety of ways. Most obviously, its imagination is put to work when it vicariously shares in the reading of *Paradise Lost,* Plutarch's *Lives,* and *The Sorrows of Werther.*[28] Of their effect on its life, the Being reports: "I can hardly describe to you the effect of these books. They produced in me an infinity of new images and feelings, that sometimes raised me to ecstacy, but more frequently sunk me into the lowest dejection."

Its active imagination causes the Being to understand the difference between "the perfect forms" of the "cottagers" (especially their "grace, beauty, and delicate complexions"), and his own form which he realized was "hideous."[29] Thus, without knowing the facts of the case, without inquiring why a man who had labored to create it would abandon it, the Being began to fabricate in imagination what it saw its position in the world to be. This view was initiated, fostered, and brought to culmination by the images of Satan in *Paradise Lost.* "Many times I considered Satan as the fitter emblem of my condition; for often, like him, when I viewed the bliss of my protectors, the bitter gall of envy rose within me."[30]

As a result of imagination Hartley's third category, ambition, comes into play. The feelings of rejection and misery give rise to the ambition to destroy the things its creator loves, and to devastate Victor's life as the Being feels its own life has been devastated. As an outgrowth of these feelings the Being murders William. When it sees the child and learns who he is, the artificial man exclaims "Frankenstein! you belong then to my enemy—to him towards whom I have sworn eternal revenge . . . I too can create desolation; my enemy is not impregnable; this death will carry despair to him, and a thousand other miseries shall torment and destroy him."[31]

The feeling of ambition is attended by Hartley's fourth and fifth categories of pleasure and pain, self-interest and sympathy, which for Hartley form the strong bases upon which man is built. He adds to these two categories "theosophy," or love of God. But in the Being's case this feeling has reversed itself and become hatred: ". . . should I feel kindness towards my enemies? No: from that moment I declared war against the species, and, more than all, against him who had formed me, and sent me forth to this insupportable misery."[32]

This hatred effectively destroys the moral sense that had been so powerful a part of the Being's early months of life. Until learning that mankind cannot bear the sight of it, the Being exudes only kind feelings. The De Lacey family is singled out for special, benevolent treatment. The artificial man not only helps them and watches over them, but says that these people "excited in me . . . various feelings of indignation, delight, and wonder . . . which all terminated in additional love and reverence for my protectors."[33]

Thus, the sensations which Hartley observes are "the impressions made on the external" initiate a range of feeling, thought, and action. This is accounted for in an elaborate account of the Being's early life and first experiences, both internal and external. Hartley believes that the seven general categories are the result of seven causes. These are:
1. The impressions made on the external senses.
2. Natural or artificial beauty or deformity.
3. The opinions of others concerning us.
4. Our possession or want of the means of happiness, and security from, or subjection to hazards of misery.
5. The pleasures or pains of our fellow-creatures.
6. The affections excited in us by the contemplation of the Deity; or,
7. Moral beauty or deformity.[34]

These seven causes give rise to their respective categories of pleasure and pain. Notice in the following sample passage how many of these causes are present.

> Of what a strange nature is knowledge! (1) It clings to the mind, when it has once seized it, like a lichen to a rock. I wished sometimes to shake off all thought and feeling (1); but I learned that there was but one means to overcome the sensations of pain, and that was death (4)—a state which I feared but did not yet understand. I admired virtue and good feelings (4 & 7), and loved the gentle manners of my cottagers (5); but I was shut out from intercourse with them (4), except through means which I obtained by stealth, when I was unseen and unknown, and which rather increased

than satisfied [the] desire I had of becoming one among my fellows (3). The gentle words of Agatha, and the animated smiles of the charming Arabian, were not for me (2). The mild exhortations of the old man (7) and the lively conversation of the loved Felix, were not for me (4). Miserable, unhappy wretch! (4, 6, 7).[35]

Against the background of Hartley's table of the sources of human pleasure and pain it is possible to see the artificial man in Mary's novel as clearly human in its nature. He is not a half-tone engraving or a puppet that imitates human actions and experiences human thoughts haphazardly or mechanically. His real tragedy is that he is endowed with a superior intensity of emotion just as he is endowed with superior size. Linked closely to Hartley is the famous statue of Condillac, another important source for the sensationalist psychology of the artificial man.

Condillac's *Treatise on the Sensations* was an attempt to make clear the theories of Locke concerning the learning process, theories which clearly attacked with vigor the theory on innate ideas.[36] However, Condillac, dissatisfied with Locke's failure to take his ideas to their logical conclusion, wrote this treatise which does exactly that.[37] The *Treatise*, as Rosenfeld points out, "exposed the weaknesses of the metaphysical attitude common to Descartes and Leibnitz, and contrasted them with the firm guidance afforded by Newton's inductive method."[38] As such, Condillac is an ideal thinker from whom to extract key ideas about the personality composition of an artificial man who was conceived and built from purely scientific principles emerging from the Newtonian method.

We know that Mary read the *Treatise on the Sensations*.[39] Rosenfeld observes that Condillac's most important contribution to the sensationalist philosophy was his awareness that while the statue remained isolated from reality and was aware of sensations alone, "the statue could very well develop a kind of rational thinking, without being aware of any relation of this thinking to an external world."[40] The moment the statue begins to touch the outside world with its senses "the spell of solipsism is broken: the thinking subject realizes that he is acting upon an external world."[41] This is precisely what happens with Mary's vision of an artificial man and its first experiences with the external world.

The artificial man is constructed in an isolated laboratory where it is denied all contact with the external world. Even when it first stirs to life, it remains passive to the environment. But the artificial man is endowed with life and thought. In effect it is a full-grown human being that has never been taught about the physical universe. Mary must have realized that she had to account for the Being learning all the necessary things about the external world it would need to know if it were to survive and become a rational creation that could communicate its thoughts to other sentient beings.

One of the most interesting things connected with the artificial man's account of its early sensations is how closely they parallel the account of the wild child found in the forests of Lithuania; a story which is recounted by Condillac in his *Treatise on the Sensations* and which serves as an important, non-theoretical example of what he has been discussing with a hypothetical statue.[42] The child, which has been reared with wolves, is brought into the world of men and taught to speak. As a result, according to Condillac, when "he was questioned concerning his former state, . . . he could remember no more about it than we can remember what happened to us in the cradle."[43] This is almost exactly the experience recounted by the artificial man to Victor at their first interview. "It is with considerable difficulty that I remember the original area of my being: all the events of that period appear confused and indistinct."[44]

The entire early history is also paralleled by the Lithuanian child's experience in that both are preoccupied by the finding and gathering of food. All else is of no consequence. "Occupied entirely in a search for food, presumably difficult to procure, it would lead a purely animal life . . . when its hunger is satisfied it will need rest. It will remain where it happens to be, its activity will be succeeded by sleep."[45] The experience of Victor's artificial man is almost identical. The picture that emerges in the artificial man's narration of its early life is one of food gathering, feeling sensations, and sleep. It only moves out of its original position in the forest because of a scarcity of food. This incident drives it into the vicinity of human company where it learns, after a long and difficult time, to speak the language of the humble cottagers near whom it is living.

Another remarkable attribute of the artificial man created by Victor Frankenstein is its penchant for thinking about all the sensations that bombard it constantly on all sides in a variety of ways. This is directly traceable to Condillac's statue that thinks about every sensation to which it is introduced, and indeed cannot, according to Condillac, do otherwise. Geraldine Carr, the translator of the *Treatise on the Sensations,* views the matter this way.

> The active posers of mind—love, hatred, hope, fear, volition—are also transformed sensations, for they follow from the fact that all experience is pleasurable or painful, and therefore, every sensation is either one we are inclined to continue, or one we seek to escape from. Thus all the powers of the mind are traced back to their origin in simple sensation. The nature of thought itself gave Condillac no trouble, it is the natural consequence of sensibility. To feel is to think.[46]

A reading of the early experiences of the artificial man shows that it is a world entirely dominated by sensation and the resultant thoughts that those sensations are constantly giving rise to. Notice in this passage how the sensations are the inevitable source of a rational course of thought as the artificial man experiences them and retells them to Victor.

> I was delighted when I first discovered that a pleasant sound, which often saluted my ears, proceeded from the throats of the little winged animals who had often intercepted the light from my eyes. I began also to observe, with greater accuracy, the forms that surrounded me, and to perceive the boundaries of the radiant roof of light which canopied me. Sometimes I tried to imitate the pleasant songs of the birds, but was unable. Sometimes I wished to express my sensations in my own mode, but the uncouthe and inarticulate sounds which broke from me frightened me into silence again.[47]

This short passage shows that it had begun to observe the external world. No longer are the sensations merely sensations which at first report were all of his experience. The artificial man is now beginning to connect sounds with objects, observing with "accuracy," perceiving the tops of the trees so that his environment has "boundaries," and finally, trying to imitate the sounds of birds and even attempting speech. As Carr has observed of Condillac's statue, "to feel is to think."[48] The two are inseparable modes of existence. Such a close parallel to the philosophy and theory of Condillac must not be accidental. An analysis of chapter three of *Frankenstein* shows that the sensationalist theory is the underlying principle beneath every thought and discovery of the artificial man's emerging consciousness. Mary has used the philosophy of Condillac and pinned it for complete exposition to the categories of Hartley. Condillac supplied the theory and Hartley the method whereby she explained the early mental life of the artificial man. It also clearly connects her to the emerging scientific attitudes of her day and shows that she was far more aware of the new science and its subsequent materialistic philosophy than has previously been thought.

Such a state of affairs separates Mary Shelley's artificial man from all the artificial humans that had been invented in myth and literature and are present in the stories of Western civilization. To indicate the wide gap that exists, I would like to very briefly examine the artificial human in literature prior to 1818 to establish three points: (1) no artificial human produced in whole or in part is as complex as Mary Shelley's artificial man; (2) the process of construction of all of these earlier artificial humans depends to some extent on supernatural means for animation; and (3) that the Being's ancestors can be generally divided into three groups—(a) the animated statue, (b) the homunculus, and (c) the automaton or robot.

From antiquity to the eighteenth century, literature has provided examples of the animated statue. This type of artificial man is exactly what its name implies: a statue which through some agency, usually supernatural, begins to move and act like a human being. I have separated this from the automaton or robot because the animated statue has no interior physiology of gears, levers, and other motivating machinery. Upon examination it is apparent that, except for outward shape and animation, they have little in common with the artificial man of *Frankenstein*.

The animated statue of antiquity is usually associated with gods and supernatural agencies. Clay figures that became men are mentioned in the myths of the Greek titan Prometheus and his Egyptian counterpart, the demi-urge Ptah. Full-size statues of solid gold are described in the *Iliad* "resembling animated youths to whom power, thought, and speech had been given."[49] Hephaestos, who created these images, is also credited with several animated statues, among them a gigantic metal colossus named Talos. Perhaps the most well-known animated statue in Greek myth is the Galatea of Pygmalion whose solid marble became flesh at a command from Aphrodite.[50]

The medieval world has innumerable examples of the animated statue also. Armed castle guards of metal are mentioned in the *Matter of Britain* and the romance of Huon of Bordeaux. Autokinetic figures are reported in *The Thousand Nights and One Night* at the court of Queen Abrizah who spoke, sang, and moved to the wonderment of the visiting Prince Sharkhan.[51] In another tale from the Scheherazade group entitled "The Ebony Horse," a human image of solid gold inlaid with jewels and carrying a trumpet is given to a Persian king name Sabur. It is to be set up as a guardian at the gate of the city and "if an enemy enters the palace, it will blow this clarion against him and he will be seized with a palsy and drop down dead."[52] Charlemagne also is reported to have seen animated statues shaped like children.[53] At the royal court at Constantinople he saw "a hundred marble columns all encrusted with fine gold, each supporting a child in bronze blowing an ivory trumpet." During a storm, the children "look at each other and laugh so naturally that you would think them all alive."[54]

The most complex of the animated statues is the clay Golem of the Jewish Hasidic mystics.[55] Chayim Bloch, the first man to make an exhaustive summary of all the stories and legends surrounding this figure, explains in great detail the method of the formation and subsequent animation of this autokinetic man. The body is crudely shaped out of clay and informed with life by employing the *Shem ha-meforasch,* "the preeminent name of God, so as to endow with life a shape" formed by the devout rabbis.[56]

The construction of the Golem is closely associated with supernatural agencies and depends for its success on the purification of the worker and a special knowledge of religious texts: "Rabbi Loew, thereupon, gave them the minutest instructions how they must before all, through deep earnest penitence, sanctify and purify themselves, in order to be prepared for the exalted work of creating a being of stone. He also pointed out to them the danger in which the three of them might be placed if, by reason of incomplete inner sanctification, the attempt would fail, for they then have used the Holy Name in vain or desecrated it."

The Golem is clearly the product of a strongly religious ceremony, whose promise of success is totally unreliable unless various arcane requirements are met and is distressingly subject to the vagaries of chance. The making of the Golem cannot be construed as a method. Success depends entirely upon intuition, devotion to God, an inner illumination bestowed upon the priest from a reading of such cabalistic writings as the *Zohar* and the *Sepher Yetzirah*, and God's will. It is far removed from the skepticism and exact repeatable process that Mary envisioned in the building of the artificial man in *Frankenstein*.

It is also apparent that the animated statue serves several functions. It can be a kind of architectural motif as in "The Ebony Horse" or the Constantinople palace. It can also be merely a cause for wonder and delight, a kind of special product that serves to embellish a story with imaginative devices as in the story of Sharkhan or in the myths of Haephaestos. Last, it is the product of divine fiat as in the animation of the figures of Ptah and Prometheus, as well as the statue of Galatea and the clay Golem. All of the animated statues are in direct contrast to the being of flesh and blood and strong emotion created by scientific principles in the laboratory of Victor Frankenstein.

The second type of autokinetic being is the homunculus. This type of artificial man is rare and is to be met with chiefly in the writings of Paracelsus and his disciples.[57] A homunculus is an artificial man cultured in vessels of glass and nurtured on a specially prepared formula of human blood. None seem to have been a full-size human being but were smaller than a human infant, although having the shape and abilities of an adult human.

Alchemical drawings often show adult female and male human beings enclosed in sealed bottles. Paracelsus himself notes that the "generatio homunculi has until now been kept very secret," and by this statement reveals himself indebted to an older tradition.[58] But he supposedly divulges this secret to the world. He gives the recipe for forming these beings out of human sperm alone in this way: "If the sperma, enclosed in a hermetically sealed glass, is buried in horse manure for about forty days, and properly 'magnetized,' it begins to live and to move. After such a time it bears the form and resemblance of a human being."[59]

This recipe is, however, by no means completely clear. If one tries to repeat the Paracelsian experiment (as one can repeat the clearly detailed experiments of Newton, Boyle, Davy, etc.) one will immediately encounter difficulties. To produce a successful homunculus it must be fed with a substance Paracelsus calls the "arcanum sanguinis Hominis," until it is at least forty weeks old. The elements of this substance are not described. The difficulty, Hartmann observes, will be overcome by the true alchemist. "To the uninitiated they [the elements] are unintelligible; while the initiated—having the light of the spirit for his teacher, will not require them."[60] So, although Paracelsus appears to give up his secret, he has really revealed nothing more than the existence of such a creation.

The homunculus clearly belongs to a different age and an entirely different set of beliefs regarding the nature of the universe than that of the Being of Frankenstein. The artificial man of the novel is described as the product of a clearly defined process which anyone possessing the careful notes Frankenstein made of his experiment could duplicate. The notes of Paracelsus reveal nothing. Only an intuitive reading can unlock the secrets of the recipe. There is also an emphasis upon the fact of the homunculi's existence as a product of a wonder-working image. Its emotional and personal life is never discussed as is the artificial man's existence in *Frankenstein*.

The third species of artificial man is by far the largest. The automaton or robot is in some respects closer to the Being in *Frankenstein* and in other more important respects quite dissimilar. An automaton by definition is a device of metal, leather, or other substance which is fashioned to look like a living creature, and which depends for its motivating power and movement on a complex inner structure of gears, wheels, and springs. This discussion will confine itself to those automata shaped into human form.

Historically, the automaton with a complex inner anatomy is a comparatively recent phenomenon. The ancients were content to visualize statues coming to life, but the age of reason seemed to demand a more satisfactory explanation. The works of Alfred Chapuis and Edmond Droz print pictures and detailed plans of dozens of automata made by artisans in the eighteenth century.[61] These automata could write letters, play pianos, walk about, play chess, and make sounds all by means of a complex, mechanical, internal arrangement. These figures were often startlingly life-like, life size, and uncannily similar to real human beings.

Mottelay's *History of Electricity and Magnetism* reports that Wolfgang von Kempelen, one of the most famous artificers, "constructed, during the year 1778 a speaking machine which 'gave sounds as of a child three or four years of age, uttering distinct syllables and words.' "[62] He also mentions the speaking head presented to the French Academy of

Sciences on July 2, 1783. Erasmus Darwin also planned a speaking head on purely mechanical principles, detailed plans for which still exist.[63]

E. T. A. Hoffmann, the German writer of fairy tales, was fascinated with human automata. In one story entitled "Automata," he gives a detailed description of an automaton that played chess. Called the Turk, "it was in fact a very remarkable automaton. In the center of a room of moderate size containing only a few indispensable articles of furniture, sat this figure, about the size of a human being, handsomely formed, dressed in a rich and tasteful Turkish costume, on a low seat shaped like a tripod."[64] The interior is also described in some detail and is just as interesting as the exterior description.

> The exhibitor would apply a key to the Turk's left side, and wind up some clockwork with a great deal of noise. Here, also, he would, if desired, open a sort of lid, so that inside the figure you could see a complicated mechanism consisting of a number of wheels; and although you might not think it probable that this had anything to do with the automaton's speech, it was still evident that it occupied so much space that no human being could possibly be concealed inside.

The fictional automaton is an average representative of the type of human simulacra popular in the eighteenth and early nineteenth centuries, and summarizes well how these inventions must have looked and felt to human sensibilities. Hoffmann wrote his entire story "The Sandman" around the mechanician/physicist Spalanzani and his fantastic automata, particularly one named Olympia that the scientist passed off as his daughter.

This female automaton, upon which he lavished twenty years of experiment, could sing an *aria di bravura* "in a voice . . . almost too brilliant, but clear as glass bells."[65] She accompanied herself upon the piano as she sang. She danced with Nathaniel, the hero of the story, but he found her touch was "cold as ice." Despite her human appearance and human actions she was "singularly statuesque and soulless. . . . She is strangely measured in her movements, they all seem as if they were dependent upon some wound-up clockwork. Her playing and singing have the disagreeably perfect, insensitive timing of a singing machine, and her dancing is the same . . . she seemed . . . to be only acting *like* a living creature."

This passage clearly underscores the difference between the automaton and the human being. Despite the perfection of an automaton's actions, they remain those of a machine. The artificial man in *Frankenstein* is a markedly different creature from the automaton. Mary Shelley's Being moves with ease and grace without a trace of clockwork action.[66] The voice is rough but human and while its general appearance is grotesque, it is more the misshapen animal rather than a cleverly constructed machine. Its emotional and psychological nature also makes it original among artificial humans. Neither the animated statue nor the automaton has an inner life, an illuminating intelligence, or a reasoning mind. Mary Shelley's artificial man embraces all three.

It is evident, then, that Mary Shelley's artificial man is a novel creation in which can be appreciated the greatest originality. It is the product of a scientific experiment, not a religious ritual, and its animation is the result of a clearly defined, repeatable, natural discovery, not a paranormal intrusion, or, as in the case of the homunculus, an enlarged human sperm that was alive to start with. It has an autonomous brain and possesses free will. It is not pre-programmed as were the robots of the eighteenth century, but learned its actions by trial and error. It possessed a clearly defined personality and although many of its physical senses are supernormal it remains, with the exception of Condillac's statue, the closest thing to a human being ever conceived of in myth or literature prior to 1818.

5

Ceremonial Magic and Alchemy

A comment frequently made about Victor Frankenstein is that he is not a scientist in the modern sense of the word but a magician and alchemist whose construction of an artificial man had a strong basis in the occult and pseudosciences. Eino Railo, for example, believes that Victor's methods are only "scientific-looking," and the room in which Victor constructs his artificial man is really an alchemist's laboratory.[1] Dr. Masao Miyoshi maintains that Victor's scientific method is "a kind of supernaturalism."[2] James Rieger indicates that the novel is "switched-on-magic, souped-up alchemy, the electrification of Agrippa and Paracelsus." Radu Florescu "concludes with Rieger" that "Mary's monster is more the child of the alchemist and occultists than of the scientist." As a result of these and similar views in the criticism of *Frankenstein,* Victor remains a man whose adherence to the "new science" of the Newtonian epoch is tenuous at best and whose research must be considered not the work of a serious scientist but, rather, the result of an alchemical experiment tinged with necromantic overtones.

An examination of the novel itself indicates that ceremonial magic and alchemy is not as omnipresent as it is usually believed to be. Part of this is the result of a misconception of both the nature of ceremonial magic and the methods and goals of the alchemical practitioner. An inquiry into the nature of both necromancy and alchemy is essential if they are to be legitimately compared with the methods and goals of the new science which permeates the book to a greater extent than is normally granted.

I would like, therefore, to examine the extent to which alchemy and the related occult arts are present in *Frankenstein* and attempt to determine the degree to which Victor may be said to be a practicing sorcerer or alchemist. To do this, I have elected to define ceremonial magic and contrast it with alchemy. Finally by dividing *Frankenstein* into sections and by applying the definitions of both ceremonial magic and alchemy to the five sections of the novel, I try to determine if Victor was a necromancer or alchemist or both and investigate to what extent these two forces really are present in his career as a scientist.

What, then, is ceremonial magic? Ceremonial magic is the attempt by a specially trained person to gain control over aspects of the environment such as weather or disease, foreknowledge of events, access to earthly riches, or other conditions on the human plane normally impossible to control by ordinary means. Control of these and similar phenomena must be obtained by paranormal means.[3]

The means were provided by a guide book of instructions discovered by practitioners in ancient times and handed down in handwritten form, or passed from adept to disciple orally.[4] These books, or grimoires, contained instructions, fully developed rituals, drawn signs, spoken phrases, lengthy and complex invocations, tools, proper costumes, and other matters by and through which the paranormal could be approached. The chief difference between the occult arts and the new science lies in the fact that any man who attempted to duplicate the experiments of a Newton, a Boyle, or a Davy would obtain the same results as they, whereas a man who wanted to duplicate the actions of the great occult adepts was not guaranteed success simply by performing a ritual and speaking the proper words.[5]

Victor discovers this truth as he attempts to perform the ceremonies of Agrippa and Albertus Magnus. When he failed to obtain the promised results, he "attributed the failure rather to my own inexperience and mistake, than to a want of skill or fidelity in my instructors."[6] Ceremonial magic was an art, not a exact science, and success depended as much upon the preparation of the student's frame of mind and the purity of his physical person as upon the ritual.

If the prescribed magical activities had been followed both explicitly and intuitively, if the magician had purified himself according to the instructions of his guide book, and if he were able to perform the ritual exactly as described with the proper intonations and intuitive insight, the desired power could be gained over the real world through the agencies of the spirit world.

An insight into this operation is provided by Manly P. Hall, himself a believer and practitioner of these matters. He contends that the "ancient art of invoking and controlling spirits" is obtained through "a scientific application of certain formulae."[7] He describes the scene in general in the following manner: "The magician, enveloped in sanctified vestments and carrying a wand inscribed with hieroglyphic figures, could by the power vested in certain words and symbols contact the invisible inhabitants of the elements and of the astral world." The successful carrying out of this process lies in the "power vested in certain words and symbols." The proper intonation of these words and the exact duplication of the symbols coupled with ritual purification and preparation of the operator was necessary if the success of the process was to be insured.

While invoking the occult powers, the magician protected himself within a circle or pentagram drawn upon the floor or ground on which were written the various names and formulae known to be able to protect the magician from the fury of the often uncooperative and dangerous elementals which the ceremony called up. When the invoked spirit appeared, it was bound by the incantatory formula to answer any question or perform any deed required of it by the magician.[8]

There is only one place in the novel where such a ceremony in the classical sense is alluded to. Victor remarks that he has performed magical ceremonies, albeit without success, in his youth after discovering the Aggripan canon while taking shelter from a storm in an inn.[9] He tells us that "the raising of ghosts or devils was a promise liberally accorded by my favorite authors, the fulfillment of which I most eagerly sought, and if my incantations were always unsuccessful, I attributed the failure rather to my own inexperience and mistake, than to a want of skill or fidelity in my instructors."[10]

A. E. Waite, who assembled the rituals of incantatory magic in a comprehensive edition, would have understood Victor's failure to achieve results. His own labors in this area were often frustrated because the grimoires which detailed the ceremonies were confused and "impossible to follow" simply because they were often incomplete or vague in their injunctions.[11]

This single reference to the raising of ghosts and devils through incantatory magic in *Frankenstein* is the only overt discussion of this matter in the novel. There are, as will be pointed out, a few other references to the ceremonies of magic and to the work of sorcerers and the raising of demons, but they are quite rare. It is not until the 1831 edition that Mary Shelley refers to her introduction to Victor as "the pale student of unhallowed arts kneeling beside the thing he had put together."[12] An examination of the novel as it was originally written, particularly the section in volume one dealing with Victor's studies at Ingolstadt and his subsequent original experiments into the secret of life, does not savor in the least of occult activities.

His inquiry into the secret of the animation of the dead leads Victor into the local charnel houses where he spends hours observing the "natural decay and corruption of the human body."[13] But this observation is free of supernatural designs or feelings. Because his father had never "impressed" his mind with "supernatural horrors" he works unafraid among these corpses with the detachment of a man to whom observation is paramount and to whom the occult is nonexistent. "I do not ever remember," records Victor, "to have trembled at a tale of superstition, or to have feared the apparition of a spirit. Darkness had no effect upon my fancy; and a church-yard was to me merely the receptacle of bodies deprived of life."[14] Such an outlook is hardly one that could be confused with the adept of arcane matters whose very success depended in no small degree on the cooperation of the spirit world and its ultimate control.

His discovery of the life-bestowing process is not tainted with magic or superstition either. "Some miracle might have produced it, yet the stages of the discovery were distinct and probable." And not only is he able to understand this process, he is able to repeat it at will. He invokes no spirit aid, draws no pentagrams, takes part in no rituals of purification, nor appeals to the instructions of the ancient magicians.

One must not confuse the natural repulsion of the human sensibilities to the stench of the charnel house and the grave with the occult. When Victor tells his story in retrospect to Walton, after his mind has been torn apart with nervous breakdown and the loss of his loved ones to the hands of the artificial man, he is still able to objectively recall the manner in which he pursued his goal and the manner in which he reacted to his success. It is not a terror of the supernatural that unseats his reason at the crucial moment of animation. It is overwork. He tells Walton that he "was oppressed by a slow fever" and that the condition was complicated when he became, as a result, "nervous to a most painful degree."[15]

The actual moment of animation is preceded by the kind of work common to the surgery or the dissecting room. No charms, no spells, no incantations or hieroglyphic wands. The candle that lights his labor is merely that, a light. It is not a ritual fire. He is surrounded by the necessary "instruments" which I infer are scientific, not magical.[16] Victor is quite familiar with scientific instruments. Not only has he been instructed in their use by his course of study at Ingolstadt, he has himself "made some discoveries in the improvement of some chemical instruments, which procured me great esteem and admiration at the university."[17] In view of these considerations, it seems hasty to imply that he was employing the methods of ceremonial magic to the construction of an artificial man. Then where does the impression that Victor is an adept of the magical arts come from?

It is quite true and demonstrable that in the rest of the novel, after his scientifically trained mind has been virtually destroyed and replaced by an abject credulity, that Victor begins to experience the shadow of the occult in his life. This casts overtones of necromancy on the novel and gives the reader a feeling that ceremonial magic is being dealt with.

Victor seldom refers to his artificial man after his nervous breakdown other than as a "daemon," a "filthy fiend," "my vampire," etc.[18] He never referred to it in these terms when he was describing his initial studies of the secret of life, or the projects that culminated in the construction of the cybernetic man. But all the epithets he applies later are terms reminiscent of the occult. He imagines that his artificial man is a creation of the necromantic arts rather than the product of a logical science. In his confused and sick mind it becomes connected with magic.

As a result, Victor sees his being as a kind of supernatural creature raised by special processes and loosed upon mankind, much as a demon raised from the infernal regions by a weak magician might escape the enchanter's power and wreak terrible deeds. Victor tells Walton that he "considered the being whom I had cast among mankind, and endowed the will and power to effect purposes of horror, such as the deed which he had now done, nearly in the light of my own vampire, my own spirit let loose from the grave, and forced to destroy all that was dear to me."[19] This estimate comes after the murder of his little brother. It is an estimate and a comparison he had up until this moment not made.

Towards the end of the third volume, in chapter seven, Mary places a scene directly connected to the tradition of ceremonial magic. Although it is not a classical evocation of the spirit world, there is no doubt of its occult roots. Victor has begun to wander about Europe, having quitted Geneva, and is attempting "to gain some clue by which I might trace the steps of my fiendish enemy."[20] He enters the cemetery where the graves of the murdered members of his family are located. The setting is well suited to the evocation of a necromantic atmosphere. The leaves of the trees are "gently agitated by the wind," and "the night was nearly dark." To his inflamed imagination "the spirits of the departed seemed to flit around, and to cast a shadow, which was felt but seen not."

Victor kneels on the grass, in itself an act denoting subservience to a higher power and with "quivering lips" delivers an invocation of his own making which is in type similar to the invocations found in the books of necromantic conjuration that had dominated his youth.

> By the sacred earth on which I kneel, by the shades that wander near me, by the deep and eternal grief that I feel, I swear; and by thee, O Night, and by the spirits that preside over thee, I swear to pursue the daemon, who caused this misery, until he or I shall perish in mortal conflict. For this purpose I will preserve my life: to execute this dear revenge will I again behold the sun, and tread the green herbage of earth, which otherwise should vanish from my eyes forever. And I call on spirits of the dead: and on you wandering ministers of vengeance, to aid and conduct me in my work. Let the cursed and hellish monster drink deep of agony; let him feel the despair that now torments me.[21]

This speech which Victor labels his "adjuration," a term directly taken from the ceremonies of magic, is clearly rooted in Agrippan sorcery.[22] Later, after following his artificial man into the wilderness, he finds "a repast prepared for me in the desert" which he believes "was set there by the spirit that [he] had invoked to aid me."[23]

The last words Victor speaks to Walton make it clear that Victor has completely reverted to his youthful studies and that the spirit of the works of Albertus Magnus and Agrippa have superseded the scientific spirit. "Ho! when will my guiding spirit," Victor exclaims, "in conducting me to the daemon, allow me the rest I so much desire. . . ."[24] He passes this task on to Walton much as an adept passes on his work to his disciple saying, "if the ministers of vengeance should conduct him to you, swear that he shall not live," a phrase reminiscent of the Biblical injunction "Thou shalt not suffer a witch to live."[25] All of these events come very late in the novel and are entirely separated from the construction of the artificial man itself.

It seems clear that the necromantic overtones of the book are concentrated in the areas of Victor's youth when he is struggling to learn the secrets of the universe, and much later in his life when his health and sanity are weakened after the arduous labor of construction of the artificial man. The area of Victor's life centered around Ingolstadt, from his introduction to the realities of scientific knowledge by Krempe and Waldman to his final construction of the artificial man, is free of any trace of ceremonial magic.

There is even less evidence of alchemy in the novel. Alchemy, as I hope to show, is not the same thing as ceremonial magic, although the two are often confused. The necromantic arts served to allow the man who had prepared himself in prescribed ways to have his wishes granted through a special ceremony which employed hidden knowledge to effect its purposes. The only tools necessary to this process were the paraphernalia of the wizard: the magic sword or staff, suitable robes, various consecrated utensils such as a brazier in which to light the sacred fire or a knife on whose blade had been inscribed various arcane symbols, and a book of instructions.[26]

Alchemy, on the other hand, operated in a much different manner and had, as a result of its philosophy, an entirely different mode of operation. In its narrowest sense alchemy is, in the words of the pseudo-Roger Bacon, "a Science teaching how to transform any kind of metall into another."[27] In its broadest sense, however, it was "thought to be the true key to Nature that would unlock the secrets of heaven and earth."[28]

As a result, three crucial differences emerge between the necromancers and the alchemists, especially in the manner in which the secrets of the cosmos were revealed. The first difference is that the alchemists did not expect an agent of the unseen, a demon or a spirit, to appear to them to which questions could be put or favors requested. Instead, the way to truth lay in the mind and understanding of the alchemist himself. A second way to truth lay through a careful reading of the Holy Scripture where, as a result of a mystical experience, a seeker might come to understand the secrets of the cosmos. A third method of discovery lay open "through . . . diligent study of nature, God's book of Creation."[29] This is a direct inquiry into the nature of Nature, based on immediate observation, not the revealed truth of ancient sages. It differs in substance from Newtonian observation in that the alchemic observation was carried out in a closed universe. The Newtonian theory and position postulated a wide, open universe.[30]

To carry out this observation of nature, the alchemist's tools were far different from those of the practicing necromancer. Here the first laboratories came into existence filled with primitive beakers, retorts, as well as bottles of "chemicals" which, when mixed together and heated, produced those substances from which the alchemist made his deductions concerning the secrets of nature. The ritualistic chant is replaced by a formula which names earthly substances obtainable by the operator which can be mixed together to obtain various mysterious compounds whose virtues were closely linked to supernatural qualities.

The alchemist is still in the direct line of the necromantic tradition in that he believed that he must be pure himself before any of his operations would work and that his activities merely readied his mind for the unfolding of revelations about the nature of the higher planes of existence. But this similarity is one of few shared by the necromancer and the alchemist; viewed together, they are very different persons.

The second difference between the necromancer and the alchemist lies in the manner in which the various activities are carried out when the investigator begins his search for truth. For the necromancer, the formulas and the rituals were already prepared in advance. It was the job of the magician to learn what these were and be able to reproduce them faithfully. If this were done, then success was assured and the sorcerer's wishes would be granted. He was in a line of ancient, prescribed magic which did not allow the slightest innovation.[31]

The alchemist, on the other hand, began with only the barest of instructions.[32] Alchemical guides such as the Emerald Tablet of Hermes or surviving, cryptic diagrams purporting to be Egyptian or Greek in origin held out the promise of success if the alchemist could fill in the sketchy outline he was given. The way to success was not exactly prescribed. All the practitioner knew was that some had achieved success using the outline, but were bound by an oath of secrecy not to pass on the details. The individual alchemist had to experiment with many substances in his laboratory trying to hit upon the right combination of substances and circumstances which would yield success. He had no prescribed rituals or formulas at his command which he might commit to memory and then reproduce in a ceremony. He was required to search for the way, and the way was closed to all except the most diligent, adept, and intelligent.[33]

It can be appreciated that this crucial difference in the method of operation sets alchemy and necromancy apart. Despite these crucial differences they are frequently confused. I believe this is true because the necromancer and the alchemist shared the same beliefs about the nature of the universe and often pursued both paths. Many of the ancient sorcerers such as Albertus Magnus and Agrippa are viewed as both magicians and alchemists. Sometimes they attempted to get at the truth necromantically, sometimes alchemically. There is no way in which the two could be joined into a single method. The confusion arises because both the sorcerer and the alchemist operated in a closed universe which had been perceived and categorized by ancient authority deriving its mandate by observation and revelation.[34]

Thus the paths of these two quite different methods met in the so-called Secret Doctrine.[35] Knowledge of this doctrine was given to only a few who could be considered worthy of receiving such knowledge. Further, the books were available to all, yet the secret knowledge they contained would only reveal itself to a master of the art who could read between the lines. The basic difference between the sorcerer and alchemist in handling the Secret Doctrine was that the former was completely imitative while the latter was contemplative.

The secret doctrine is closely bound up with the alchemical notion of the changes that matter undergoes as it is heated in the alchemical fire. This process of transmutation is symbolic of the transmutation of the soul and the understanding of the alchemist who performed the operations. The mystical relationship of the operator to his operations is seen, for example, in the early alchemists of all countries. The death of the substances in the alchemic fire symbolized the worldly death of the operator, just as the dross in the crucible is transformed into the gold of the human being (i.e., the perfection of the individual man). "In man, the alchemist induces in his own person a similar separation of spirit from gross matter. In this case the result is a perfected person."[36] There is no mention of this in *Frankenstein*.

The most obvious (and only) correlation between Victor and the alchemists lies in his youthful search for the elixir of life and the philosopher's stone. The works of Agrippa and Albertus that he read provoked his curiosity until he "entered with the greatest diligence into the search of the philosopher's stone and the elixir of life."[37] Both of these are purely alchemic studies and are not in any manner related to the pursuits of ceremonial magic.

The philosopher's stone was perhaps the most important aspect of the alchemist's studies. The philosopher's stone promised undreamed of wealth to the man who discovered how to make it. Its single property and sole ability was the transmutation of any baser substance to pure gold unalloyed by dross of any kind.

> The achievement of the Stone was the great and final goal of alchemy. In its fullest aspect, the quest was dominated by a singularly noble ideal, for it was imperfect man's search after perfection. To most of its seekers, however, the Grand Magisterium and Elixir was merely a magic source of wealth, health, and long life. "Gold," says Goethe, "gives power; without health there is no enjoyment, and longevity here takes the place of immortality." With such considerations in mind, and inspired by their vivid faith in the miraculous virtues of the imaginary Stone, generation after generation of alchemists during an epoch of more than a thousand years, devoted their lives and treasures to the pursuit of the greatest *ignis fatuus* which the world has ever known.[38]

The ingredients of the stone were unknown and it was to this end that the copious records and numerous recipes that form so much of the literature of the alchemists were written. However, if the ingredients were unknown, the method by which success might be achieved was not. Since alchemy was "the art of separating the pure from the impure" the alchemist was concerned with the arts of refinement of all substances he worked with.[39]

An outgrowth, almost a consequence of the search for the philosopher's stone, was the investigation of substances that might yield the elixir of life. It is to this end that Victor is drawn in his youthful researches. The elixir of life, Victor records, "obtained my most undivided attention: wealth was an inferior object; but what glory would attend the discovery, if I could banish disease from the human frame, and render man invulnerable to any but a violent death!"[40]

Mary says nothing about the acquisition of the necessary laboratory instruments to carry out these researches although she must have known they were needed. We evidently are to assume that Victor had the means to acquire them just as he obviously had the leisure to pursue such studies. There is no doubt that he understood that the Elixir of Life (or the Grand Elixir as it was sometimes called) was a "panacea for all human ills, capable also of restoring youthfulness and prolonging life."[41] These two references remain the only overt references to alchemy in the entire novel.

It is difficult to understand how Rieger could assert that the science of Victor Frankenstein was "switched-on alchemy" or the "electrification of Agrippa." There is no hint in the careful preparations Victor performed in the assembling of this artificial man's component parts that he attempted to keep himself pure in the ritualistic sense or that he believed in the necessarily closed universe of the alchemists. Alchemy, in order to function, needs a closed universe, otherwise the symbolism of the Secret Doctrine will be worthless.

Victor indicates his loss of faith in alchemy when his father "constructed a small electrical machine and exhibited a few experiments" and further "made . . . a kite with a wire and string, which drew down the fluid from the clouds."[42] As a result of this demonstration of new science and its learning, he was cured of his idolatry of the ancient triumvirate. "This last stroke," Victor says, "completed the overthrow of Cornelius Agrippa, Albertus Magnus, and Paracelsus, who had so long reigned the lords of my imagination." He "considered" his authors "useless whom the professor had so strongly reprobated." He understands that "the ambition of the inquirer seemed to limit itself to the annihilation of those visions [upon] which my interest in science was chiefly founded. I was required to exchange chimeras of boundless grandeur for realities of little worth."[43] These statements make it very clear that he no longer believes in the possibilities of sorcery and alchemy. Victor's retreat to an attic room and his nocturnal collecting expeditions are not alchemic but dictated by necessity, as will be shown in the last chapter. Why should we attempt to read otherwise?

There is another manner in which one can see that the alchemy working in the life of Victor Frankenstein is clearly separated from the Newtonian scientist. The essential clues to this clear separation of science and magic/alchemy and the rejection of the charge that Victor is a magician and alchemist lies in the structure of the novel itself.

If the novel can be considered a biography of the artificial man as well as of Victor Frankenstein, the novel is clearly divided into five parts distributed among three volumes. Part one is introductory in nature and epistolary in form (as are all the sections). It introduces the reader to the narrator of the story, the scientist-explorer Robert Walton, through whose letters will be revealed the history of Victor Frankenstein. It is in this section that the reader gets his first glimpse of the artificial man through the eyes of the scientifically minded Walton who is engaged at the moment on an exploration of the Arctic region to determine the validity of the myths surrounding the circumpolar area. Walton decides to serve as Victor's emanuensis. He "resolved every night, when I am not engaged, to record, as nearly as possible in his own words, what he related during the day."[44] In this introductory set of letters, as previously pointed out, there is no reference to the occult.

Volume one rehearses the biographical history of Victor Frankenstein. It is here that we find the single reference to his experimentation with ceremonial magic and alchemistry. But when Victor is sent to Ingolstadt to pursue a study of natural philosophy all references to ceremonial magic cease. I consider this part two of the story as it recounts to the reader the formation of the mind of the artificial being's maker. He clearly rejects the works of Albertus Magnus, Paracelsus, and Agrippa in favor of men who wrote and experimented with the new science. "From this day," Victor tells Walton, "natural philosophy, and particularly chemistry, in the most comprehensive sense of the term, became nearly my sole occupation. I read with ardour those works, so full of genius and discrimination, which modern inquirers have written on these subjects. I attended the lectures, and cultivated the acquaintance, of the men of science of the university . . . the more fully I entered into science, the more exclusively I pursued it for its own sake."[45]

Part two is brought to a close with the construction and animation of the artificial man (its "birth"), which brings to a close the history of Victor Frankenstein as a student and practitioner of the new science.

Part three begins almost immediately after the animation episode. The artificial man is temporarily forgotten as Victor slowly recovers his health and sanity, returns home, and enters into family relationships again totally devoid of references to the artificial man or to alchemy, sorcery, or science. With the murder of Victor's brother, William, a new note enters the novel, almost imperceptible but definite in its sinister assertion.

The Being is to be blamed for this murder and the story rapidly moves to the heart of part three which is a lengthy autobiography of the Being told in retrospect in its own words. This section, which occupies nearly the whole of volume two, is, with the exception of Victor's interspersed references to his daemon and fiend, devoid of references to the occult. Part three moves to a swift climax in which the Being warns Victor in a speech which prepares us for the sinister activities of the artificial man in the fourth section.

Victor rejects (possibly through his own biased emotional state generated by the murder of his brother at the hands of his own creation) the possibility that the artificial man can act in a benevolent manner and in so doing completes the destruction of the benevolent psyche of the artificial man. One of the ironies of the novel is the beautiful inner nature of the artificial man which stands out in sharp contrast to the deformed exterior. Victor cannot accept the artificial man's true self because he is unable to equate an ugly body with a beautiful soul. As a result, Victor's harsh words to his creation complete the psychological destruction his initial abandonment of it began. Victor's words are harsh. Despite the revelations in the artificial man's own words of its tortured inner personality, Victor's own psychological problems and his inability to cope any longer with any problem in a purely objective manner mask the truth from him. He is no longer a scientist, merely a man suffering from the critical effects of a recent nervous breakdown and subsequent ill-health. Victor tells his creature, "you swear . . . to be harmless; but have you not already shewn a degree of malice that should reasonably make me distrust you? May not even this be a feint that will increase your triumph by affording a wider scope for your revenge?"[46]

This speech is one of the most critical for the interpretation of the novel. It is evident that at this point in the story the majority of critics side with Victor and see the artificial man as a "monster" whose word is unreliable. But as Swingle has shown there is some doubt about this.[47] Mary has devoted nearly a third of her novel to an explanation of the artificial man's inner personality, in the most sympathetic terms, which I see as an attempt to show that the Being, despite his malformed exterior, possesses a personality that is fragile and in need of objective aid. The entire section is a great cry for help from the Being. Its animation is but the start of a long process that begins on the floor of Victor's attic laboratory.

The Being's first gropings with reality, its self-education in learning to use its body as well as its self-taught efforts in reading and the use of logical processes, are unparalleled. I have already pointed out how this relates to Condillac and Hartley. The Being has given evidence of being extraordinarily intelligent, yet it needs help and understanding to become a complete intellectual being which Victor, engrossed in his own problems and suffering from an intellect impaired by grief and nervous disorders, is unprepared and unable to give.

The artificial man's speech that immediately follows Victor's rejection shows that Victor has created the final overthrow of the Being's psychological nature. He has destroyed every benevolent and gracious trait of its finely tuned personality. "How is this?" the artificial man exclaims,

> I thought I had moved your compassion, and yet you still refuse to bestow on me the only benefit that can soften my heart, and render me harmless. If I have no ties and no affections, hatred and vice must be my portion; the love of another will destroy the cause of my crimes, and I shall become a thing, of whose existence every one will be ignorant. My vices are the children of a forced solitude that I abhor; and my virtue

will necessarily arise when I live in communion with an equal. I shall feel the affections of a sensitive being, and become linked to the chain of existence and events, from which I am now excluded.[48]

Part three ends with this pronouncement. It is paradoxical that Victor, who had discovered the manner of bestowing life on inanimate flesh, has no ability to bestow the real life which the Being so passionately begs him to grant. At this point of the story, so crucial to an understanding of the novel, there are three points of view that can be adopted. One must side with Victor, side with the Being, or take an impartial view wherein Victor is not Mary's exclusive spokesman, but her example of folly and misunderstanding. I believe that Mary's view is much broader in context than the mad, broken viewpoint of a Victor Frankenstein.

Part four of the novel is devoted to a recounting of the criminal deeds of the Being. The troubles of Victor Frankenstein, brought on since he has turned away from the cool, rational world of science and adopted the old, hysterical attitudes of prejudice and superstition, reach a hysterical climax in a series of related deaths and end with a chase that leads both Victor and his Being into the northern regions far from the habitations of men, where brute nature in its most primitive state serves as background for the climax of the novel. It is this section that utilizes the terms and attitudes of the sorcerer and marks a return to Victor's early belief in Agrippa.

Part five brings the book full circle and is devoted to the last days of Victor, his death, and the promise of the self-immolation of his artificial man. It is, except for references to the Being as a demon and fiend, free of alchemic or necromantic overtones. The cold wastes of the Arctic furnish a dismal and cruel backdrop against which the final scenes are acted. It is most important because it is here at the very end of the novel that we meet the artificial man face to face for the second and last time and hear him speak to us through the ears of Walton.

In the light of this evidence it seems wrong to continue to see Victor as an alchemist or as a magician. The strong overtones of magic that the names of Albertus Magnus, Agrippa, and Paracelsus give off are excluded from those sections of the novel where the scientific education and subsequent researches of Victor Frankenstein are set forth. Isolation from one's fellows, researches that are conducted in the night hours, or even the seasonal grimness of November when the artificial man is animated are not in themselves related to the supernatural, to magic, or to alchemy.

6

Use of the New Science in *Frankenstein*

There can be little doubt that it was the new science and its methods which inspired *Frankenstein*. This chapter will discuss the role the new science played in the novel. I will define as clearly as possible what the new science was, and compare the methods and theories of the new science with those found in the novel itself.

The new science was a technique for investigating the physical nature of the universe.[1] It was based on the supposition that the structure of the universe was knowable by man through the careful application of human reason to the observation of natural phenomena. Roger Cotes, in the preface to the second edition of the *Principia,* enunciated its basic principles in this manner: "They proceed . . . in a twofold method, synthetical and analytical. From some select phaenomena they deduce by analysis the forces of nature, and the more simple laws of forces; and from thence by synthesis shew the constitution of the rest."[2] This statement clearly indicates that the new science promoted a rational skeptical attitude from which truth could be discovered with more certainty than through the oracular method favored by some two thousand years of magic and pseudoscience as the road to knowledge.[3]

In the methods of new science, any hypothesis that was selected for study was subjected to the rigorous trial of experiment. An experiment was an artificial method for observing some natural phenomenon under tightly controlled conditions. An experiment was usually conducted a number of times, and if the same results were obtained each time under identical conditions, then an inference could be drawn.

This inference, arrived at by means of the analogical method, could then be used to derive a law about the manner of operation of an extremely isolated and limited bit of natural phenomena. Rule two of Newton's method of natural philosophy is firm in its statement that "to the same natural effect we must, in so far as possible, assign the same natural causes."[4] Sir Humphry Davy in his *Elements of Chemical Philosophy* explained the process by which an investigator could arrive at truth in this way. "The foundations of chemical philosophy are, observation, experiment, and analogy. By observation facts are distinctly and minutely impressed on the mind. By analogy, similar facts are connected and by experiment new facts are discovered; and, in the progression of knowledge, observation, guided by analogy, leads to experiment, and analogy confirmed by experiment, becomes scientific truth."[5]

Diderot, in his *Thoughts on the Interpretation of Nature* (1754), one of his most important statements on the subject of the new science, echoed Davy's opinions in this manner: "We have three principal methods at hand: the observation of nature, reflection, and experiment. Observation gathers the facts; reflection combines them; experiment verifies the result of the combination. The observation of nature must be assiduous, reflection, profound, and experiment, exact. The three methods united in one person are rarely seen. Hence creative geniuses are not common."[6]

It can be readily appreciated that the new science embraced principles that admitted only the most exact information as the basis for the formation of statements about the nature of the universe. Nothing was taken for granted. There was no appeal to authority except the authority of reason as it directed the human senses which in turn observed the result of a carefully controlled investigation. A man no longer needed to depend upon the findings of past authority.[7] Authority was suspect because its knowledge was often derived from an opinion arrived at through the reasoning process alone without reference to what might actually take place.[8] As a result of this practice of ignoring what actually took place, "the most refined doctrines . . . concerning natural causes . . . were little more than a collection of vague speculations, rather poetical than philosophical."[9]

The scientific method as outlined above can be seen operating in a variety of places in *Frankenstein*. The scientific method is inherent in Victor's career as both a student and as a practicing scientist. As pointed out in the last chapter, he is not in any way an alchemist, as is so often charged, in his post-graduate career. Victor's whole scientific career (which effectively ends when he succumbs to a species of paranoia and abandons his artificial man to the vagaries of chance) is based on the scientific method.

The methods of the new science can be first discerned in Victor's childhood when he is drawn to the study of the secrets of the universe. However, he is completely ignorant of the methods by which his age had learned to deal with the problems of the universe and was, through chance, brought under the guidance of men of an earlier time and their philosophies. The science of Agrippa and Paracelsus was too closely related to a closed world view to be of any real value to him.[10]

But despite this erroneous tutelage from the dead, useless masters, Victor possesses within himself a natural ability to think and act upon his own. At this stage of his life the scientific method is latent which later his inclination towards discovery in the natural world will release little by little. He begins to apply (although he does not as yet know that is what he is doing) the principles of observation to the simple everyday things in his environment that cause him to wonder about the causes of natural phenomena. "The natural phaenomena that takes place every day before our eyes did not escape my examinations. Distillation, and the wonderful effects of steam, processes of which my favourite authors were utterly ignorant, excited astonishment; but my utmost wonder was engaged by some experiments on an air-pump, which I saw employed by a gentleman whom we were in the habit of visiting."[11]

He exhibits here a predisposition to throw off the yoke of ignorance, realizing that despite the fame with which the names of his teachers are surrounded they are ignorant of the mundane things which are the province of the scientist. If he can see these natural but minute aspects of nature, untutored as he is, how much more to the discredit of the ancient experts that they make no mention of them. Such reflection "served to decrease their credit with me."[12] Victor goes on to say that despite this shortcoming he "could not entirely throw them aside" because they at the time were the only minds and systems of which he had knowledge. But he clearly indicates that if "some other system should occupy their place in [his] mind" he would be willing to replace his early idols.[13]

Such a statement is not conjecture or idle talk. Shortly after he makes this observation, Victor sees a display of natural electricity that completely destroys "an old and beautiful oak." He is clearly not satisfied with any answer that he could obtain about the nature of thunder and lightning from Paracelsus, Agrippa, or Albertus Magnus and goes instead to his father for a more satisfactory explanation.

His father employs an explanation from the discoveries of the new science, calling the force "electricity" and describing the "various effects of that power" with scientific analogies. "He constructed a small electrical machine, and exhibited a few experiments; he made also a kite, with a wire and string, which drew down that fluid from the clouds."[14] There lies in this illustration an implicit truth that is often ignored.

The recognition that lightning is electricity was not made clear until Franklin and others had experimented with this force and determined there was no difference between them; that electricity was, in fact, produced by lightning and that lightning was ungoverned and uncontrolled electricity.[15] In his history of electricity Priestley devotes an entire chapter to this matter entitled "Dr. Franklin's Discoveries Concerning the

Similarity of Lightning and Electricity." Priestley remarks that "the greatest discovery which Dr. Franklin made concerning electricity, and which has been of the greatest practical use to mankind, was that of the perfect similarity between electricity and lightning."[16]

We are therefore given two ideas here about new science which are often overlooked. The youthful mind of Victor Frankenstein is focused through this incident upon the failure of the ancients to provide a satisfactory answer for phenomena as common as thunder and lightning. He is, further, treated to a small lecture in which the latest bits of scientific knowledge about the subject are revealed. At the conclusion of this illustration, his old gods are dead. "This last stroke completed the overthrow of Cornelius Agrippa, Albertus Magnus, and Paracelsus, who had so long reigned the lords of my imagination."[17] Other discoveries in the field of electricity are present in the novel.

Of interest in this connection is the "small electrical machine" constructed by Victor's father. Priestley devotes a lengthy chapter to descriptions of various electrical machines then in vogue and compares them with others made before his time.[18] He notes that the earlier machines, especially those made by the Abbé Nollet and Hauksbee were made of wheels "exceedingly large, and the frame of the machine proportionably strong."[19] In using the word "small" to describe the size of the electrical apparatus constructed by Victor's father, Mary Shelley is, it seems to me, making us aware that she is fully aware that electrical machines came in assorted sizes and that some were, in Priestley's words, "more fit for a large laboratory than a private study."[20] Furthermore, she indicates that she is aware that it was then the fashion to construct such pieces of equipment for private amusement and instruction.

In his chapter on "Branches of Knowledge of Use in Electricity" Priestley discusses the relative ease with which such machines could be constructed. Electrical machines were supplied and repaired by the makers of mathematical instruments but Priestley encouraged the scientist to make his own. "It were much to be wished," he observed, "that philosophers would attend more than they do to the construction of their own machines." Evidently, such machines were novelties to the educated class who could perform "common experiments" with such pieces of equipment.

This shows that Mary is aware of a number of problems of the new science as applied to the relatively new field of electricity: lightning and electricity are seen to be one and the same; the famous Franklin experiment with a kite is mentioned; small pieces of electrical apparatus are constructed at home for experiments; and an awareness of a power in nature that is not magical but natural, that man can understand and in some measure control, are all implicit in the passage. But most important of all, this clearly separates the old dualistic attitudes held by Agrippa and others from the new, monistic attitudes that became popular with the advent of Newton.[21] Mary indicates to us that she is fully aware of one of the most celebrated experiments on electricity in her day and its application to the study of the universe.

She makes her positive attitude toward Newtonian science more clear when she sends Victor to the University of Ingolstadt to study natural philosophy. It is at Ingolstadt that he will develop his early proclivities for observation and precocious experiment that characterized his early years and will continue to characterize his student career. Ingolstadt was a Jesuit school famous for its investigations and innovative attitudes and was considered a "center for science."[22]

The University of Ingolstadt offers the student of natural philosophy a course of study whose underlying base is Newtonian science. When M. Krempe, the first professor of chemistry that Victor meets, discovers that he has spent his time studying Agrippa, etc., Krempe bluntly tells him he has been "studying . . . nonsense."[23] Victor learns in his first lesson about the new science that he lives in "an enlightened and scientific age" and that the "fancies" that he had "so greedily imbibed, are a thousand years old, and as musty as they are ancient."[24] Victor rapidly learns that the new philosophy produces men who do not seek "immortality and power" but, rather, had set about "annihilation of those visions" which held sway for many thousands of years in man's history. But it is in the chemist M. Waldman that one hears the Newtonian note most strongly.

Waldman is not as cruelly blunt as Krempe in his assessment of such men as Albertus Magnus, Agrippa, and Paracelsus. He is aware that while they "promised impossibilities, and performed nothing," they were nevertheless, "men to whose indefatigable zeal modern philosophers [are] indebted for most of the foundations of their knowledge."[25]

In this first meeting with Victor couched in the form of a lecture "upon modern chemistry" Waldman provides a serious summary of some of the achievements of modern science.

> The modern masters promise very little; they know that metals cannot be transmuted, and that the elixir of life is a chimera. But these philosophers, whose hands seem only made to dabble in dirt, and their eyes to pour over the microscope or crucible, have indeed performed miracles. They penetrate into the recesses of nature, and shew how she works in her hiding places. They ascend into the heaven's, they have discovered how the blood circulates, and the nature of the air we breathe. They have acquired new and almost unlimited powers; they can command the thunders of heaven, mimic the earthquake, and even mock the invisible world with its own shadows.[26]

It is still unclear whether Mary herself believed that what Waldman told Victor was a true state of affairs and that Waldman and Krempe were the spokesman of her own point of view. Perhaps it will prove impossible to bring enough evidence to bear on this problem of who serves as Mary's spokesman in the novel. Some of the problems attendant upon this difficulty have been considered at length by L. J. Swingle in his discussion of the novel and its relationship to certain problems of knowledge.[27] Who are we to believe, he asks, the monster or Victor? "Experience," Swingle points out, "serves to render more complex the question of the monster's nature and to confuse the attempt to decide whether the creature can be trusted. Like other Romantics of her generation, Mary Shelley shows that experience may multiply rather than answer questions."[28]

But while it is perhaps impossible to discover whose point of view Mary herself believes in, such a state of affairs argues that a writer who would present multiple answers to questions must know the facts that go along with those questions if both sides are to be presented in proportion. Mary's summary of scientific success has as a result more weight. For each one of the statements presents clearly Mary's knowledge of a major breakthrough for science; let us now analyze Waldman's summary in detail.

The philosophers who "dabble in dirt" are those minds who have begun to examine the real universe, that is, the ordinary environment. The physiologists for example had begun to investigate the human body as a mechanism thanks to the mechanistic arguments of La Mettrie, Condillac, and others. This permitted precisely the same objectivity that Victor evinces when he begins his investigation of the cause of the spark of life by examining corpses without fear of the supernatural or disgust.

Morbid anatomy was even in Mary's time being advanced to very high levels of knowledge by such men as Bichat who for all practical purposes established through his studies of tissues (both macroscopic and microscopic) the principles of modern histology.[29] Bichat's work, which resulted in his *Treatise on Membranes* (1799–1800), studied twenty-one specific tissues and remains today a model of scientific detachment and clarity of explanation. Men such as Malpighi of Bologna used the microscope to observe the lung tissues of a frog and helped Harvey to understand that the blood circulates.[30] Malpighi was one of those who were able to "penetrate into the recesses of nature, and shew how she works in her hiding places."[31] Dampier observes that it was Malpighi "who gave the first description of the microscopic changes which convert an opaque white spot in the egg into the living bird."[32] Their eyes have indeed seen the real miracles of the environment and have published their reality so that any man can also see and understand. Such knowledge is not reserved for a privileged few who have the time to develop an imprecise art. Malpighi and others were able to show, as Mary expressed it, how nature works "in her hiding places."

She also is aware of man's experiments with lighter-than-air craft. Man's first ascent into the heavens was accomplished by J. F. Pilatre de Rozier, who remained aloft for four minutes in a balloon built by the Montgolfier brothers and later floated for five and one-half miles across Paris.[33] Wolf records that "during the years following 1873, numerous balloon flights were undertaken all over Europe, many of them involving novel and spectacular features."

The "nature of the air we breathe" had been under investigation for a long time.[34] Before Lavoisier, investigators such as Hales discovered how to collect and store various types of "airs." Black was interested in analyzing the air that caused suffocation in deep mines. Priestley made great advances in pneumatic chemistry and Darwin himself was involved in investigating the subject. Wolf shows a variety of apparatus used by and developed by Priestley to make several major contributions to the study of gases. By Mary's day much had been learned about the composition of the atmosphere.[35] She demonstrates to us that she knows about these matters because she provides Victor with some experiments on an air pump. Davy specifically mentions the air pump in a historical view of chemistry in his *Elements*.[36]

The "new and unlimited powers" which she writes about cannot be definitively named but there lies within the phrase a feeling that Mary knows and to some extent shares the optimism of the scientists of her day that science will show man the way to knowledge and truth and make him master of the universe. The eighteenth century was a fertile ground for advances of every kind, and an inquiring and curious mind such as that possessed by Mary Shelley would have been impressed with these advances. The use of gunpowder for blasting and warfare would indeed seem to mean that man could "command the thunders of heaven," and the shaking of the earth in such operations would "mimic the earthquake."[37]

The most curious reference in this paragraph is the manner in which science can "mock the invisible world with its own shadows." I presume that she was referring to the magic lantern and its permutations that were currently the rage in Paris and elsewhere on the Continent.[38] In 1794 a Belgian optician named Etienne-Gaspard Robertson devised a spectacular show with his "ghost-making machine" as he phrased it.[39] "Summoned by the conjuror, phantoms of Voltaire, Mirabeau, Jean-Jacques Rousseau, Robespierre, Danton, all appeared and faded away again 'into thin air.' Great credence was given to Robertson's ghosts and it was to be some years before his secret use of concave mirrors and convex lenses, concealed assistants and props was revealed."[40] Despite the supernatural effects Robertson obtained, it was his earlier work in the science of optics which enabled such a show to succeed.

The magic lantern was public knowledge. A medical doctor named Hooper, who was a contemporary of Mary, published a four volume work in which the magic lantern was described and the various effects of which it was capable were detailed.[41] Hooper calls the magic lantern a "very remarkable machine, which is now known over all the world." He gives minute details of its construction and devotes several chapters to the effects it is possible to present with this early projector.

The work is divided into chapters called "recreations." In recreation twelve, which was entitled "To Produce the Appearance of a Phantom, upon a Pedestal Placed on the Middle of a Table," the mechanical aspects of the picture reproduced in Haining's book are given in detail.[42] Basically, a magic lantern was fastened to the bottom of a table fitted with a glass top. The cone of light thrown by the lantern was reflected by an inclined mirror inside the table "in such a manner that it may pass out at the aperture made in the top of the box."[43] If a glass slide is introduced between the light source and the mirror on which "may be painted a spectre, or any other more pleasing figure," a most unusual effect is produced.[44] The smoke of the light source was channeled up through the table along with the image so that the image appeared in three dimensions on the table top amid the smoke.[45] There were ways to make the image appear to move. Hooper remarks that "tho' we have mentioned a small magic lantern, yet the whole apparatus may be so enlarged, that the phantom may appear of a formidable size."[46]

A solar microscope such as was owned by Shelley and used by him for various scientific inquiries at Oxford is a kind of magic lantern that uses the light of the sun as its source of illumination.[47] The barrel of the microscope is fastened into a window that can be completely draped and thus darken the room. Various objects can be introduced into the microscope between two pieces of glass and the image projected onto a wall or piece of white paper.[48] "A small insect, such as a flea for example, may be made to appear as large as a sheep, or a hair as large as a walking-stick; by means of this instrument the eels in vinegar, or flour paste, will have the appearance of small serpents."[49] Living slides will continue in this device to move until the heat of the sun kills them. Such devices were improved upon by such men as Etienne-Gaspard Robertson who substituted living actors for the glass slides and was able to reproduce life-size "ghosts" for credulous audiences.

That paragraph with its hidden depths of scientific knowledge reveals that Mary Shelley in all probability knew much more science than she has been given credit for. The materialism which had infiltrated science, and was its major philosophical stance, is found in the paragraph and elsewhere as well. She seems to handle such ideas with consummate ease. This list of scientific achievements is struck off her brain without effort.[50] I submit that only a person who is well-versed in her subject could write so off-handedly about scientific achievements. Compressed into that one paragraph is at least two centuries of learning beginning with Galileo and ending with Davy. Mary also shows us that she is familiar with the university and the curriculum it offered, particularly in science.

Waldman, as a representative of the University of Ingolstadt, for example, shows that it is far different from other European centers of learning. A critical estimate of Alexander de Laborde's five volume *A View of Spain* that appeared in the *Edinburgh Review* in 1809 shows that Ingolstadt, even in the eighteenth century, was well-established as a center of learning in the new science and is in sharp contrast with its Spanish counterpart.[51] Laborde writes that

> such are the establishments in Spain for the advancement of science: in number fully adequate to the wants of the nation; but in spirit, activity and acquaintance with modern discoveries, miserably deficient. Their schools of astronomy are destitute of instruments and observatories; their courses of natural philosophy are without experiments; their teachers of natural history are unfurnished with cabinets; their professors of anatomy give no demonstrations; their schools of chemistry are without laboratories and apparatus; and their libraries of learning are destitute of modern books.[52]

Mary gives us a school that is the equal of the splendid medical universities of Edinburgh or Paris and uses a university in Germany that was well-known for its curriculum in the new science. Ingolstadt has been transformed from the kind of school current in seventeenth-century Germany which specialized in occult matters. It has converted its curriculum to scientific matters. Thorndike has shown that the dissertations and disputations favored in the seventeenth century were heavily in favor of the supernatural aspects of the universe and did not concern themselves with scientific investigations.[53]

While themes suggested by Cartesian materialism are investigated by students, they are clearly in the minority when one compares them to the enormous number of academic articles devoted to occult matters. Tobias Tandler, a professor at Wittenberg in 1613, published five dissertations dealing with physical-medical matters.[54] Yet the emphasis of these articles is upon the magic, not the science, despite a certain "commendable skepticism." In 1605 Tandler "contributed to the volume [on medicine] a dissertation . . . on fascinum and incantation, an oration on specters delivered on the occasion of conferring the M.D. on Peter Schmilaverus in

1608, on the question of divination and other marvelous effects of melancholy persons by a boy. . . ."⁵⁵

Mary shows us Ingolstadt, a typical German university of a century later in which the curriculum has been reformed and drastically changed. Science and all of its related subjects have taken over. Krempe makes it quite clear that the study of supernatural ideas or the studies of Paracelsus and Agrippa which had been common a century earlier had become anathema. When Victor reveals that he spent youthful hours studying Agrippa and the like, Krempe tells him, "you have burdened your memory with exploded systems, and useless names. Good God! in what desert land have you lived, where no one was kind enough to inform you that these fancies, which you have so greedily imbibed, are a thousand years old, and as musty as they are ancient."⁵⁶

In drawing a picture of the academic world into which Victor Frankenstein finds himself involved, Mary shows herself and her information to be accurate. Newtonian science and the subjects which came from it are taught, but, more importantly, are depicted as being believed in as the sole, modern method of philosophical belief. Victor discovers at the outset of his stay at Ingolstadt that his studies are out of fashion and that a new, potent force has replaced them with a far more accurate method of discovering the secrets of the universe and of controlling the power that the universe has to offer man. At this point, at Ingolstadt, Victor trades sorcery for chemistry.

It is difficult to know exactly what Mary meant by the term "chemistry" but it is safe to assume that she drew some of her knowledge of it from Davy.⁵⁷ In his *Elements of Chemistry* which she read and studied, Davy defines chemistry as "changes, whether natural or artificial, whether slowly or rapidly performed."⁵⁸ "The object of Chemical Philosophy," Davy believes, "is to ascertain the causes of all phenomena of this kind, and to discover the laws by which they are governed." Victor employs this philosophy and the method implicit within it when he begins his studies of human physiology.

Victor is attracted to the problem of how the human frame was "endued with life."⁵⁹ In order to observe this phenomenon, he tells us that he "must observe the natural decay and corruption of the human body." His inquiry is tinged with chemical overtones in the Davy sense of the word. For Davy, chemistry was a process of discovering how the products of matter broke down into component parts. Part one of his *Elements* begins with a chapter entitled "On the Laws of Chemical Changes; on Undercompounded Bodies and Their Primary Combinations."⁶⁰

It seems entirely possible that Mary, having read Davy at length, came to certain conclusions about how a scientist such as Victor would have proceeded in his investigations of the manner in which the human frame was animated. She shows Victor, therefore, engaged in a process of examination of the human body in as minute detail as possible to get an ordered picture of the whole before he will be able to begin the process of creation in reverse order.

It seems highly unlikely that he would have been able to obtain bodies for his experiments.[61] Only a limited number were made available, usually bodies of executed criminals, to designated specialists who performed their dissections publicly in a theater surrounded by medical students.[62] Although necropsy was practiced and even flourished in the eighteenth century, it was not subject to public approval and in many cases was practiced only because the general public was ignorant of the nature of scientific dissection of the human form. Dickens's *A Tale of Two Cities* set in the eighteenth century shows the figure of Jerry Cruncher, a "resurrection man" carrying on his surreptitious trade in the most clandestine manner.[63] Even Bichat, at the height of the Reign of Terror, when the bodies of executed aristocrats were treated with contempt, had to be supplied his cadavers by license.[64]

Much has been made of Victor's clandestine operation—observing in the charnel house the progressive decay of cadavers in order to learn the inmost secrets of the human frame—as a questionable, even horrible occupation, a sure illegitimacy of his pursuit.[65] But Mary presents this aspect calmly and in a detached manner. There is no hysteria or horror. "I do not ever remember to have trembled at a tale of superstition, or to have feared an apparition or a spirit," Victor tells us.[66]

His investigation is of the highest scientific order. He calmly goes about his tasks in the charnel house, patiently observing and making analogies before putting his new knowledge to the test of experiment. Despite the fact that he was "forced to spend days and nights in vaults and charnel houses," and that his "attention was fixed upon every object the most insupportable to the delicacy of the human feelings," he views the human body in decay as merely "food for the worm." "Darkness," he tells Walton, "had no effect upon my fancy; and a churchyard was to me merely the receptacle of bodies deprived of life." Such a view is entirely consistent with the philosophy of La Mettrie who viewed the body as a mechanism only. When the vital spirit was extinguished, life stopped.[67] A human body that had ceased to function was no more to be feared than a machine that had ceased to operate. Victor gives evidence that he was patterned after the extreme materialists of the eighteenth century in his attitude here.

There is not a trace of superstitious feeling or of horror in the entire passage relating his early observations. Like da Vinci before him, forced to spend his nights in the morgues of Italian cities drawing the decaying interiors of human forms by candlelight because he could not view these bodies by day in a proper laboratory, Victor maintains scientific detachment and interest in his subject.[68]

This observation carried out by Victor so that he might experiment with the spark of life and its cause is entirely consistent with Davy's point of view. In Davy's introductory lecture to the chemistry of nature delivered January 31, 1807, he says:

> The most acute and penetrating genius, unassisted by scientific methods, wholly fails in its attempts to trace effects to their causes; and an acquaintance with the minute relations and properties of natural objects, and the laws by which they are governed, can be obtained by philosophical study only; by an inquiry into natural science, into that system of extensive knowledge which has been accumulated in different times, and collected *from a variety of sources, by multiplied observations, labour, and ingenuity.*[69] [emphasis mine]

This is exactly Victor's method in the charnel house. He tells us that his method was to examine and analyze "all the minutiae of causation, as exemplified in the change from life to death, and death to life...."[70] Davy in the lecture referred to above tells us that progress in natural science "is founded on minute critical views of the general order of events taking place upon our globe."[71] Mary shows us Victor taking part in such activities with enthusiasm and a thorough knowledge of the scientific process.

The mechanistic nature of Victor's experiments are made quite clear at the end of his investigations into decay when the secret of life becomes clear to him. "Some miracle might have produced it," he says, "yet the stages of the discovery were distinct and probable."[72] In a lecture on electro-chemical science, Davy remarked in a similar spirit of inquiry, that "one order of events flows from another, an immense number of phenomena depend upon a single law, but all may be considered as a work of mechanism."[73]

A modern scientist would feel that Victor's investigation is rather crude, mixing chemistry with physiology irresponsibly and ignorantly. But the time in which these experiments and observations were made had not yet formed the nice distinctions of the twentieth-century sciences.[74] Of this problem, S. E. Toulmin has observed that "before Lavoisier set out his ideas, the criteria for marking off chemical substances from other sorts of things were extremely vague, and different scientists were inclined to include in the list of substances some or all of a wide range of things which we would exclude."[75] Toulmin believes that "there was great obscurity about the distinction between chemical processes and physical ones: the more often that light, for instance, was thought of as a substance, the more tendency was there to treat optical phenomena as effects of combination and decomposition."

Vartanian tells us that La Mettrie believed in a process similar to that in which Victor is shown as acting. "Behind the conception of a work such as La Mettrie's *L'Homme plante* (1748) was the assumption, consciously applied, that the whole of Nature presents a uniformity and continuity, a series of unbroken steps from the simplest organisms to the most complex."[76] Victor's remarks to Walton show that Victor has acted in a similar manner with a similar philosophy in mind. His discoveries might have been the product of "some miracle" but "the stages of the discovery were distinct and probable."[77]

The exact kind of chemistry or physiology employed by Mary Shelley in her view of Victor's experiments is beyond the knowledge of this writer and outside the purposes of this study. Schofield has pointed out the numerous schools of thought operating in eighteenth-century England and the Continent that derived their inspiration from Newton.[78] Arnold Thackray in his essay on Newtonian matter-theory and the development of chemistry has observed that the difficulties of arriving at a coherent and definitive view of chemistry in the eighteenth century would be an almost impossible task.[79] "The period witnessed," he points out, "the crucial stages in the transformation of chemistry from a motley collection of unconnected, and often contradictory, clusters of knowledge held by disparate social groups, into a coherent, professionalized and autonomous science."

Mary was not in a position to be a practicing chemist, but she was in an excellent position to understand its theory. In Byron's Diodati quarters she was daily subjected to the intense conversations of Byron and Shelley. The latter, had he not been expelled from Oxford, perhaps might have become a research chemist.[80] Grabo remarks on Shelley's ability as a scientist. "The degree to which Shelley was a scientist in the modern meaning of the term is difficult to decide. His actual experimentation seems to have been restricted to his earlier years before he devoted himself to reform and to have been limited to chemistry and electricity. But he evidently continued to be widely read in scientific philosophy and to the last found in it suggestion and inspiration for poetry."

Present also at these conversations was John Polidori who had just recently graduated from a medical school in Edinburgh. Rieger refers to Polidori as a "first-rate" physician "fresh out of Edinburgh."[81] Rieger believes that Polidori, who received his degree in medicine when he was nineteen, even then quite young for such an accomplishment, "must have shown extraordinary talent and promise to have been recommended by

Sir Henry Halford to an international celebrity like Byron the following year." A person who was so well-grounded in contemporary science must have been able to teach Mary some of the concepts and theory of eighteenth-century science when she needed help and clarification. What she could not get from Shelley, who was in Rieger's words an "accomplished chemist," she could have made up by "consulting with Polidori."

The Newtonian unwillingness to accept another's word about scientific matters without proper proof can also be seen in the character and studies of Walton who narrates the story of Frankenstein. He is on a voyage of discovery (a scientific matter) to the Arctic regions in order to discover once and for all whether the legends that have intrigued man about the polar regions are true or false.[82] To prepare himself for this expedition he has studied "mathematics, the theory of medicine, and those branches of physical science from which a naval adventurer might derive the greatest practical advantage."[83] The important thing to remember about Walton is that he is a skeptic who wants to prove for himself in order that he might believe. He does not go to ancient authority, he goes to the object itself and observes in order that he might draw an accurate conclusion.

It seems very clear from this evidence that Mary presents Victor Frankenstein, Robert Walton, Krempe, and Waldman as proponents of "a physical world governed by laws ascertainable by the human mind." These laws were to be discovered, not by a priori reasoning, not by some reference to an authority, such as the ancient philosophers, or the Scriptures, but by "empirical means."[84] In both method and attitude the new science made itself felt in *Frankenstein* and displaces the old systems of thought.

There remains one more matter to discuss in relation to the scientific theory which served as a background to the novel. It is usually assumed that Mary conceived of the construction of an artificial man on scientific principles in isolation, and that there were no precedents to Victor's experimentation with reviving the human frame. I believe that there was ample precedent in scientific circles and that Mary must have been aware of this activity.

By the eighteenth century a considerable body of anatomic knowledge had been accumulated, most of it through direct observation of, and experimentation with, human corpses.[85] Among this international set of anatomists there were the Germans J. E. Jerbonstreit, L. Heister, Friederich Hoffmann, and George Ernst Stahl, the Swiss Albrecht von Haller, the eminent Dutchman Hermann Boerhaave, and the astonishing and influential Johann Wilhelm Ritter.[86] Of this group Ritter and the school of *Naturphilosophes* may have been most influential in Mary's novel.

Walter D. Wetzels in his article on natural science in German Romanticism has demonstrated that the Romantics were particularly drawn to the Schlegel-Novalis circle who gave rise to a "Romantic biology," a "Romantic physics," and a "Romantic physiology."[87] There is no record that Percy Shelley and his circle knew about Ritter, but the reference at the outset of *Frankenstein* to "German physiologists" who had provided the germ of the idea for the story, a work closely allied with Romantic physiology, provides a link in inference if not in fact.[88]

Notice that in the introduction to the third edition Mary Shelley has repeated not only the name of Darwin in the same context as in the earlier introduction, attributed to Shelley, but she has augmented the passage with a further reference to galvanism.[89] Mary reports that the Diodati circle "talked of the experiments of Dr. Darwin, . . . who preserved a piece of vermicelli in a glass case, till by some extraordinary means it began to move with voluntary motion. Not thus, after all, would life be given. Perhaps a corpse could be re-animated; galvanism had given token of such things; perhaps the component parts of a creature might be manufactured, brought together, and endued with vital warmth." Wetzels points out that the *Naturphilosophes* and particularly Ritter were fond of this type of thought. They "revealed from the very beginning," Wetzels says, that they were "avid experimenters" and along with it were visionaries "with a definite predeliction for quasi-poetic amplification of experimental data."[90]

It was with galvanism and its implications for human physiology that Ritter spent most of his life experimenting. His "earliest experimental work concerned the physiological effects of galvanism" and experimented with both living and dead humans. One of his concerns, for example, "was to explore the effects of galvanism on human sense organs."[91]

Ritter was himself but one of several experimenters of the time who were fascinated with the powers of electricity and its effect upon animals and the human body. Giovanni Aldini, the nephew of Galvani, had experimented upon corpses in 1804.[92] In these experiments the corpse was convulsed by electrical current. The muscles were affected by this current to such a degree that the bodies sat up and performed other simple muscular tasks. Mottelay reports that contemporary accounts show that "in the experiments which Aldini made during 1804, the body became violently agitated and even raised itself as if about to walk, the arms alternately rose and fell and forearm was made to hold a weight of several pounds, while the fists clenched and beat violently the table upon which the body lay. Natural respiration was also artificially reestablished and, through pressure exerted against the ribs, a lighted candle placed before the mouth was several times extinguished."[93]

The previous year Aldini had experimented upon the corpse of a hanged murderer named Forster who, after being exposed to the cold air at Newgate for at least an hour, was subjected to the "precise effects of galvanism with a voltaic column of one hundred and twenty copper and zinc couples."[94] This experiment was public knowledge, being published in a number of scientific journals of the day and in Aldini's own "Essai theorique."[95] The *Edinburgh Review* noticed a book published in English by Aldini on this and other experiments on corpses although they were not enthusiastic about science using dead humans to carry on such research.[96] "M. Aldini," they reported, "has often performed his processes on the dead human subject; but the accounts that he gives of his results, are rather more disgusting than instructive."[97] They refer specifically to the experiment on Forster by Aldini, remarking that in the book by Aldini, translated by an unknown editor, was an appendix "containing an account of some experiments made by M. Aldini on a malefactor executed at Newgate; a detail of experiments of a similar kind made at Bologna. . . ."[98]

In the same year (1803) Dr. J. C. S. Carpue repeated Aldini's experiment on the body of an executed murderer, Michael Carney.[99] Carpue was trying to ascertain whether a powerful electrical current could revive a corpse immediately after execution. Carney's body was taken to the operating theater immediately following his execution. A tracheotomy was performed and three pints of oxygen were pumped into the lungs through a pipe. Simultaneously the phrenic nerve was electrified. The experiment was a failure. Despite the contraction of the right auricle no other strong movements could be induced, possibly because the current was not powerful enough.[100]

De la Rive reports that Aldini also electrified the heads of oxen and other animals which had been recently decapitated.[101] His strong electrical currents caused life-like reactions: "the eyes were made repeatedly to open and roll in their orbits while the ears would shake, the tongue move and the nostrils dilate very perceptibly." Such activity adds unexpected depth to Victor's struggles to learn the secret of the spark of life as he "tortures the living animal to animate the lifeless clay."[102] The convulsive propensity of electricity on dead frogs and other animals is echoed in the first "convulsive motion" that "agitated the limbs" of his artificial man.[103] Perhaps the "instruments of life" that Victor used to "infuse a spark of being into the lifeless thing that lay at [his] feet" were electrical instruments.[104] The words "convulsive" and "spark" seem to have greater significance in the light of these electrical experiments than mere fortuitous choice of words.

All of this indicates that the use of human bodies, while unacceptable and discomforting to the general public, was not at all unusual among such scientists as Aldini. One of his contemporaries, a highly skilled and well-known French anatomist and physiologist, Xavier Bichat, notes in his book on human anatomy that he often used the corpses of those executed to conduct experiments and did so without any qualms.[105] In his *Recherches physiologiques sur la vie et sur la mort* (1800) he dissected over 600 bodies in less than six months.[106] In his book he says "I had authority, during the winter of the year 7 (1798) to make different experiments upon the bodies of those guillotined. They were at my disposal thirty or forty minutes after the execution. In some, every species of mobility was extinct; and in others this property was restored with greater or less facility in all the muscles, by common agents. It was developed, particularly in the muscles of animal life, by galvanism."[107]

In the light of this contemporary research it can be appreciated that while Victor's researches appear to be singular and unique, the studies going on in the late eighteenth and early nineteenth century at the highest levels shows that such was not the case. The use of human bodies to ascertain whether or not electricity was the source of the spark of life was, while not common, still done and knowledge of such things could very well have been a part of the discussions at Diodati.[108] This is particularly true since Polidori had so recently graduated from the medical schools at Edinburgh and would have of necessity been familiar with all the latest research.[109] It is quite possible that the experiments of Ritter, Aldini, and Carpue, as well as those of Bichat served as precedents which Mary used in fashioning her novel.[110]

The assembly of the body of the artificial man from component parts is also regarded as a distinct, creative innovation by Mary Shelley. It has, to my knowledge, never been pointed out that much work had been done in this area on the production of artificial human body parts, and even the assembly of human bodies made of wax that could be assembled and disassembled at will.[111]

Pierre Joseph Laurent, a French engineer, fashioned a mechanical arm capable of movement in various directions for the Duc de la Vrillière.[112] We also know that various technicians made artificial legs which could assist the patient in climbing and descending stairs, and which could bend at both the knees and ankles at the desire of the wearer. Even arms and hands, articulated to move in subtle and lifelike ways, were invented and in use in the eighteenth century.

The creation of human organs and other body parts in wax was not unknown.[113] Mademoiselle Biheron (1719–1786), who was a friend of Diderot, a Paris native, and the daughter of a surgeon, devoted forty-seven years to a study of anatomy and the replication of body parts in wax. In the *Mémoires* of the Comtesse de Genlis we are told that her masterpiece was a female body which could be opened and dismantled for inspection.[114] McCloy reports that "she modeled her anatomical parts after cadavers that she kept in a glass cabinet in her garden." So lifelike were the representations that the Scottish surgeon Sir John Pringle is said to have remarked that all they lacked in being natural "was the stink."[115]

It is not possible to tell with certainty if Mary read the *Mémoires* of Mme. de Genlis. Pollin has pointed out that Mary owned the *Nouveaux Nouvelles* of de Genlis and that he "assumes" that she read the Pygmalion story from this work "before the evening of her inspirational nightmare."[116] However, her depiction of Victor Frankenstein's study of corpses in order to learn not only the causes of life but also to study the intimate details of human physiology, from which he began to construct his own artificial man, is strikingly similar to the activities of Mademoiselle Biheron and a parallel not to be overlooked. Mary's chief innovation in these matters is making Victor use parts of animals and men rather than wax. But it must be noted that these did not furnish all of the components exclusively. Mary tells us that the dissecting room and the slaughterhouse furnished only "many" of the materials for the body of the artificial man, not all. Perhaps he used other substances. Mary is not specific.

From the evidence cited it appears certain that Mary knew more about the new science than she has been given credit for, and that she must have been more aware of scientific developments, experiments, theories, and activities than the book discloses. The hints in the text, and the many concurrently published records of scientific studies and achievements, show that while hers was the first novel that attempted to use this science as the basis of a full scale story, the information upon which it is based was not the fabrication of a young and impressionable girl making up a story cut from the whole cloth of a nightmare. Like all good novels of speculative fiction, hers was an extrapolation of known facts moved into unknown and unproven areas. The metaphysical facts of the novel are so closely tied to the physical that it is difficult to separate them. Perhaps that was her intention. The fact remains that she used a strong scientific basis for the novel and as such there is reason for calling it, as Aldiss does, the first novel of speculative fiction.[117]

7

Conclusion

Mary Shelley's *Frankenstein* has proved more durable than the first critics imagined it would be. Subsequent analyses of the novel have shown that it is far more complex than a superficial reading indicates, and that complexity lies in several directions, none of which have priority or are mutually exclusive. This study has examined an aspect of the novel that has never been fully looked into: the use of the new science as a major force in the book. The results of the research suggest several conclusions.

First, criticism has generally concentrated on the moral fable that *Frankenstein* represents and has ignored the problem of the science as a side issue. With the emergence of speculative fiction as a legitimate area of concern for critics in the academic arena, *Frankenstein* must be evaluated in an entirely new light as an early work of this genre. The great number of literary offspring which the book has been responsible for, and the increasingly popular use of the phrase "Frankenstein's monster" as a general term for the identification of the irresponsible use of scientific achievement, forces the novel into a new category. As a result, its underlying intellectual structure needs to be exposed if a deeper, more penetrating understanding is to become possible, and the science upon which it is built is to be identified.

Clearly the artificial man in *Frankenstein,* while part of a general species that has been frequently presented in Western literature, has special qualities that set it apart from all of its forbears. It seems to be a fictionalized account of Condillac's statue. The statue is drawn out of a work of pure theory and thrust into a world of action and experience. Thus, the implications of Condillac's statue are made even more clear.

Although Victor Frankenstein has often been associated with sorcery and has been evaluated as a scientist who adopted the methods of alchemy to achieve his aims, I believe the evidence is sharply against such a view. Sorcery and alchemy figure very little in the novel. I have indicated that while the atmosphere of the book is one of fear and horror, this must not be confused with the adoption and the use of Newtonian science as a positive, creative force. Newtonian monism lies at the heart of *Frankenstein,* and it is from this concept that the book conceived by Mary Shelley gains its strength.

Victor Frankenstein rejects sorcery and alchemy as successful ways of understanding the environment and controlling it. Through a series of incidents Mary shows her main character being introduced to the new science. She shows how he is educated in this scientific philosophy at a leading university, and indicates that he is so successful in his studies that he decides to perform a daring experiment, i.e., learn the secret of the animation of the human form. He succeeds, but has a failure of nerve and mind at the crucial moment. The experiment turns against Victor, and plagues those he loves as well. All of the plot structures and major incidents of the novel are substantially supported by the Newtonian philosophy exemplified in the life, schooling, and experiments of Mary Shelley's hero and scientist, Victor Frankenstein.

Notes

Notes for Chapter 1

1. Mary Shelley, *Frankenstein, the 1818 Text,* ed. James Rieger (Indianapolis, 1974), p. xxvii. Unless otherwise noted, all references to *Frankenstein* will be taken from this edition.

2. Carl Grabo, *A Newton Among Poets* (New York, 1968). See particularly chapter two, "Erasmus Darwin: I. General Scientific Ideas," pp. 30–59. About Shelley's use of scientific ideas, Grabo has remarked: "For his most finely spun imaginings there is yet usually some scientific justification. To assume of a line of Shelley's verse that beneath its highly wrought dress there is no hard core of intellectual meaning, is to miss almost inevitably its true significance" (p. 35).

3. See also Carl Grabo's *Prometheus Unbound, An Interpretation* (Chapel Hill, N. C., 1935) where he discusses other aspects of this idea. Grabo believes that "the importance of Newtonian theory to Shelley is evident."

4. This attribution is found in a number of places. See *Quark: A Quarterly of Speculative Fiction,* eds. Samuel R. Delany and Marilyn Hacker, No. 1 (November 1970), p. 7. Both editors are experts in the field of speculative fiction.

Notes for Chapter 2

1. The criticism presented in this chapter is the most complete list of articles and books written about *Frankenstein* compiled in any bibliography to date. I have excluded any discussion of ephemera which number in the thousands. I presume that there are articles that have escaped my notice but I have endeavored to be as complete as possible.

2. I have cross-checked my list of early reviews with Reiman's exhaustive reprints of contemporary reviews about Romantic publications. See his *The Romantics Reviewed* (New York, 1972). I have included a discussion here of the *Edinburgh Magazine*'s review of *Frankenstein* which was not in Reiman. I have preferred, wherever possible, to use the primary source.

3. This review was reprinted in the *Critical and Miscellaneous Essays of Sir Walter Scott, Collected by Himself,* vol. one (Philadelphia, 1841). All page references here to his review on *Frankenstein* in *Blackwood's* will be taken from this reprint.

4. I have been unable to locate a copy of this review. The quotations here are reproduced in both R. Glynn Grylls's study *Mary Shelley: A Biography* (London, 1938), and Christopher Small's full length study entitled *Mary Shelley's Frankenstein: Tracing the Myth* (Pittsburgh, 1972). It is not in Reiman.

5. Small, *Tracing the Myth,* p. 20; Grylls, *M. Shelley: A Biography,* p. 316.

6. Reiman, *The Romantics Reviewed,* pp. 41–45.

7. *The Quarterly Review* 18 (January 1818), p. 385. The vitriolic outburst of the *Quarterly* is savage. Elsewhere in the review they referred to the novel as "a tissue of horrible and disgusting absurdity" (p. 382).

8. Helen Moore, *Mary Wollstonecraft Shelley* (Philadelphia, 1886). The relevant *Frankenstein* material is found in chapter seven. Her review is really extraordinary, surveying the novel with the eye of an appreciative connoisseur. It is pleasant to read and often quite objective, showing at several points a mind that thought for itself.

9. Mrs. Julian Marshall, *The Life and Letters of Mary Wollstonecraft Shelley,* 2 vols. (London, 1889). This was the first authoritative life. Much of the information in it has remained essentially unaltered. Her style of presentation is scholarly, presenting the material with great objectivity.

10. Lucy Maddox Rossetti, *Mrs. Shelley* (London, 1890). She relies heavily on Mrs. Marshall's work and material, but the book was written to cater entirely to a popular curiosity.

11. Mary Wollstonecraft Shelley, *Tales and Stories,* ed. Richard Garnett (London, 1891).

12. Edith Birkhead, *The Tale of Terror: A Study of the Gothic Romance* (London, 1921). This book is in some ways very dated because so much has been written in the genre itself since the book was published. At the time the book was published it was almost the only work on the subject.

13. Eino Railo, *The Haunted Castle* (New York, 1923).

14. Ibid., p. 309.

15. Richard Church, *Mary Shelley* (New York, 1928). The book is little more than an extended meditation on the meaning of Mary's life as it is exposed in her fiction. It is of little major importance.

16. Grylls, *Mary Shelley: A Biography.* This is the first thorough and nearly complete biography of Mary. Grylls confines herself mostly to matters of biographical fact and makes few critical remarks on the literary works.

17. Ibid., p. 319.

18. Milton Millhauser, "The Noble Savage in Mary Shelley's *Frankenstein.*" *Notes and Queries* 190 (June 1946): p. 248.

19. Muriel Spark, *Child of Light* (Essex, 1951).

20. Muriel Spark, "Mary Shelley: A Prophetic Novelist," *The Listener,* February 22, 1951, pp. 305–6.

21. Louis Awad, "The Alchemist in English Literature. Part I. *Frankenstein*," *Bulletin of the Faculty Arts, Fuad I University of Cairo* 13(1951): 32–82. A valuable, concise history of autokinetic beings in Western literature. In his discussion of *Frankenstein*, however, Awad assumes that Percy Shelley, not Mary wrote the book.

22. Elizabeth Nitchie, *Mary Shelley* (New Brunswick, N. J., 1953).

23. Ibid., pp. 26–27.

24. M. A. Goldberg, "Moral and Myth in Mrs. Shelley's *Frankenstein*," *Keats-Shelley Journal* 8 (Winter 1959). Dr. Goldberg, Assistant Professor of Literature at Antioch College, has contributed several articles to the field of Romantic criticism.

25. Eileen Biglund, *Mary Shelley* (London, 1959).

26. Lowry Nelson, "Night Thoughts on the Gothic Novel," *Yale Review* 52 (December 1962). Mr. Nelson is author of *The Baroque Lyric* and teaches comparative literature at the University of California at Los Angeles. The *Yale Review* offers an intellectual potpourri on a diverse number of matters.

27. James Rieger, "Dr. Polidori and the Genesis of *Frankenstein*," *Studies in English Literature* 3, No. 4 (Autumn 1963). Dr. Rieger has devoted his scholarly life to an analysis of this and other novels of Mary Shelley. He is the leading authority on both Mary and *Frankenstein*.

28. Ibid., p. 466. See Mary Shelley's introduction to the 1831 edition in Rieger's edited text version, p. 222 ff.

29. Mary Graham Lund, "Shelley as Frankenstein," *Forum* 4 (Fall 1963). This article is virtually worthless as a serious consideration of the novel. *Forum* is published at the University of Houston as an interdisciplinary journal of general, not scholarly, interest.

30. Mary Graham Lund, "Mary Godwin Shelley and the Monster," *University of Kansas City Review* 28, No. 4 (Summer 1962). This journal presents a variety of original verse, stories, and literary criticism. Its ostensible purpose is to foster a reflection of "our contemporary world" as it is seen in literature both past and present.

31. Mary Shelley, *Frankenstein*, eds. R. E. Douse and D. J. Palmer (London, 1963). Their introduction is general but precise, containing the standard ideas elegantly presented.

32. Harold Bloom, "Frankenstein, or the New Prometheus," *Partisan Review* 32, No. 4 (Fall 1965). This is a thoughtful reconsideration of the Promethean element in the novel by a well-known critic of the Romantic Movement. The essay was originally written for the New American Library, Signet Edition of *Frankenstein*, and appeared as the afterword.

33. Burton R. Pollin, "Philosophical and Literary Sources of *Frankenstein*," *Comparative Literature* 17, No. 2 (Spring 1965). This journal in its own words "provides a forum for those scholars and critics who are engaged in the study of literature from an international point of view." Dr. Pollin's article is a fine example of the high standard maintained by this journal.

34. Ibid. I have retained Dr. Pollin's pagination in this quotation whose source is the J. M. Dent edition of *Frankenstein* (London, 1912).

35. Stephen Crafts, "*Frankenstein*: Camp Curiosity or Premonition?," *Catylyst*, No. 3 (Summer 1967). I hesitate to take much stock in Mr. Crafts's analysis of the novel as he is neither a literary authority nor does he provide a view of *Frankenstein* as a literary critic. However, he does see the novel from a sociological angle, amplifying in some respects ideas Millhauser discussed. *Catylyst* is published biennially by New York University at Buffalo. Their credo is expressed this way: "It is addressed to those who are seriously concerned with understanding the structure of human societies and the major problems they face. It is not merely attempting to reflect on intellectual revolution but to bring it forth." Its writers are both practicing professionals and students.

36. P. D. Fleck, "Mary Shelley's Notes to Shelley's Poems and *Frankenstein*," *Studies in Romanticism* 6, No. 4 (Summer 1967).

37. William Beckford, *Vathek,* translation with an introduction by Herbert B. Grimsditch (London, 1948), p. 125. Quoted by Fleck, p. 244.

38. See Shelley's "Alastor," 11.20–23.

39. E. Nageswara Rao, "The Significance of *Frankenstein*," *Triveni* 37 (October 1968).

40. Masao Miyoshi, *The Divided Self: A Perspective on the Literature of the Victorians* (New York, 1969), p. 80. Dr. Miyoshi teaches at the University of California at Berkeley.

41. Milton Mays, "*Frankenstein*, Mary Shelley's Black Theodicy," *Southern Humanities Review* 3, No. 2 (Spring 1969), p. 146.

42. Sylva Norman, "Mary Wollstonecraft Shelley," in *Shelley and His Circle,* ed. Kenneth Neill Cameron, vol. 3 (Cambridge, Mass., 1970).

43. Mary Shelley, *Frankenstein,* ed. M. K. Joseph (Oxford, 1971). This edition of the novel uses the edition of 1831 as the basis for its text. Next to Rieger, it must be considered the authoritative text of the novel.

44. Robert Kiely, *The Romantic Novel in England* (Harvard, 1972). An entire chapter is devoted to a consideration of *Frankenstein,* pp. 155–73.

45. Aija Ozolins, "The Novels of Mary Shelley: From *Frankenstein* to *Falkner*." An unpublished dissertation, University of Maryland, 1972. From the abstract.

46. Noel B. Gerson, *Daughter of Earth and Water: A Biography of Mary Wollstonecraft Shelley* (New York, 1973).

47. Martin Tropp, "Mary Shelley's Monster: A Study of Frankenstein." An unpublished dissertation, Boston University, 1973. From the abstract.

48. Patrick J. Callahan, "Frankenstein, Bacon and the Two Truths," *Extrapolation* 14, No. 1 (December 1972). Patrick Callahan teaches at the University of Notre Dame in the Department of English. *Extrapolation* is published at the College of Wooster. It is the first journal to devote itself exclusively to the problems of speculative fiction, inviting scholars of note to express their views on aspects of the field. It is under the general editorship of Dr. Tom Clareson.

49. Mary Shelley, *Frankenstein, the 1818 Text,* ed. James Rieger (Indianapolis, 1974), pp. 48–49.

50. Brian Aldiss, *The Billion Year Spree* (New York, 1973), pp. 7-39. See especially chapter one: "The Origin of the Species." Mr. Aldiss is a noted writer of speculative fiction. His book is the first attempt to offer a kind of history of speculative fiction covering specific areas of the genre. It is written from the viewpoint of a professional writer of speculative fiction who enjoys the literature. It is personal rather than objective in style and lacks documentation.

51. Small, *Tracing the Myth*. This book was first published in England by Victor Gollancz Ltd. in 1972 under the title *Ariel Like a Harpy: Shelley, Mary and Frankenstein*. Mr. Small is literary editor and drama critic of the *Glasgow Herald*.

52. William A. Walling, *Mary Shelley* (New York, 1972).

53. Shelley, *The 1818 Text*.

54. Ibid., p. xxvii.

55. Ibid.

56. Radu Florescu, *In Search of Frankenstein* (Boston, 1975).

Notes for Chapter 3

1. Mary Shelley, *Frankenstein*, Bodleian MS, Abinger 63. I would like to thank Lord Abinger for his kind permission to quote from the manuscript. I would also like to thank the Custodians of the Duke University Library for their help in providing me with copies of the manuscript on microfilm in their collection.

2. Mary Shelley, *Frankenstein, the 1818 Text*, ed. James Rieger (Indianapolis, 1974).

3. The most authoritative text of *Frankenstein* is that of M. K. Joseph (Oxford, 1971).

Notes for Chapter 4

1. Mary Shelley, *Frankenstein, the 1818 Text*, ed. James Rieger (Indianapolis, 1974), p. 49.

2. Ibid., p. 51.

3. Ibid.

4. Ibid., p. 10.

5. Ibid. For a similar, contemporary expedition see the lengthy account recorded as *The Private Journal of G. F. Lyon of H. M. S. Hecla*. Originally published in London in 1824 and reprinted by the Imprint Society (Barre, Mass., 1970). Lyon commanded the discovery ship Hecla "on an expedition in search of the Northwest Passage under the orders of Captain (afterwards Sir) William Edward Parry" (p. x).

6. I regard this to be an extremely significant point. Mary seems to be making a clear effort here to contrast the lucid mind of Walton with the distraught and precariously balanced perceptions of Victor.

7. Shelley, *The 1818 Text*, p. 17.

8. No study has as yet been written of the relationship of vocabulary to the depiction of character in *Frankenstein*. In my mind, Victor's generally cool appraisal of his education and his post-graduate experiments begin to become hysterical with the

words "Who shall conceive the *horrors* of my secret toil, as I *dabbled* among the unhallowed damps of the grave . . ." (p. 49) [emphasis mine]. Even in retrospect he seems to be recreating for Walton his physical and mental deterioration.

9. Shelley, *The 1818 Text*, p. 216.
10. Ibid., p. 49.
11. Ibid., pp. 52, 216.
12. Ibid., p. 109.
13. Ibid., p. 49.
14. Ibid., p. 46.
15. Ibid., p. 47.
16. Ibid., p. 49.
17. The use of live animals for experiments was commonplace. Vivisection often combined with electrification was a common practice. See Part I of Galvani's *De Viribus Electricitatus in Motor Musculari Commentarius* (Cambridge, Mass., 1953) for his experiments with electricity on live frogs. Also see Bichat's *Physiological Researches on Life and Death* for his experiments on live animals. "For this purpose, I opened the jugular and the carotid of a dog: the one furnished me with a certain quantity of black blood which, received in a bottle filled with oxygen, became immediately a shining purple; I injected it by the artery; but the animal died suddenly, and with promptitude which I had not before observed" (p. 201). Even a casual perusal of Priestley's *History of Electricity* (New York, 1966) will reveal numerous examples of the electrification of plants and animals.
18. Shelley, *The 1818 Text*, p. 52.
19. Ibid.
20. I have used a reprint of this work found in *Backgrounds of Romanticism: English Philosophical Prose of the Eighteenth Century*, ed. Leonard M. Trawick (Bloomington, 1967), pp. 51–105.
21. For an account of this see Thomas Jefferson Hogg, *The Life of Percy Bysshe Shelley*, introd. Edward Dowden (New York, 1906), p. 359.
22. Sir William Cecil Dampier, *A History of Science and its Relations with Philosophy and Religion*, 4th ed., postscript one. Bernard Cohen (Cambridge, Mass., 1966), p. 198.
23. Shelley, *The 1818 Text*, p. 52.
24. La Mettrie for instance believed that "thought is so little incompatible with organized matter, that it seems to be one of its properties on a par with electricity, the faculty of motion, impenetrability, extension, etc." Julien Offroy de la Mettrie, *Man a Machine* (La Salle, Ill., 1912), pp. 143–44. This is the only translation of La Mettrie's 1798 version available in English. See Blair Campbell's discussion of this complex subject in his "La Mettrie: The Robot and the Automaton," *Journal of the History of Ideas* 31, No. 4 (1970), pp. 555–72. Campbell points out that "motion is universal, conceptual, predictable and therefore necessary: the soul functions consequently upon the same principle as the most insignificant dust particle. Knowledge is universal since knowledge must be of motion and man is unified" (p. 561).

25. Trawick, ed., *Backgrounds of Romanticism*, p. 53.
26. Shelley, *The 1818 Text*, p. 97.
27. Ibid., p. 99.
28. Ibid., p. 123.
29. Ibid., p. 109.
30. Ibid., p. 125.
31. Ibid., p. 139.
32. Ibid., p. 138.
33. Ibid., p. 117.
34. David Hartley, *Observations on Man, His Frame, His Duty, and His Expectations*, facsimile reproduction of 1749 ed. (Gainesville, Fl., 1966), p. 3.
35. Shelley, *The 1818 Text*, p. 116.
36. Étienne Bonnot, Abbé de Condillac, *Treatise on the Sensations*, trans. Geraldine Carr (Los Angeles, 1930). This is the only complete translation of the *Treatise* in English.
37. See Geraldine Carr's introduction to her translation of the *Treatise*, p. xxii. "His main point of departure from Locke is in his theory that there are not two sources of ideas, sensation and reflexion, but only one, sensation, and from this alone is derived the whole nature of the activity which characterizes mind. He criticizes Locke for not carrying the natural method of analysis far enough."
38. L. Rosenfeld, "Condillac's Influence on French Scientific Thought," in *The Triumph of Culture: 18th Century Perspectives*, eds. Paul Fritz and David Williams (Toronto, 1972), p. 162. With the exception of scattered remarks about Condillac, Rosenfeld's essay is one of two devoted exclusively to Condillac and his thought. Dr. Rosenfeld is a teacher of nuclear physics at the Teoretisk Atomfysik in Copenhagen.
39. Radu Florescu, *In Search of Frankenstein* (Boston, 1975), p. 171. Also see the numerous lists of Mary's reading for the years 1816 and 1817.
40. Rosenfeld, "Condillac's Influence," p. 163.
41. Ibid.
42. Condillac, *Treatise on Sensations*, pp. 224–27.
43. Ibid., p. 225.
44. Shelley, *The 1818 Text*, p. 97.
45. Condillac, *Treatise on Sensations*, p. 224.
46. Ibid., p. xxiv.
47. Shelley, *The 1818 Text*, p. 99.
48. Condillac, *Treatise on Sensations*, p. xxiv.
49. Homer, *The Iliad*, introd. Gilbert Highet (New York, 1950), p. 347. The myth is recounted in Book 18. See also Louis Awad's account of this matter in "The Alchemist in English Literature," p. 34.

Notes for Chapter 4

50. See Pollin's discussion of the relationship of the Pygmalion myth as retold by Mme. de Genlis and Mary Shelley. Burton R. Pollin, "Philosophical and Literary Sources of *Frankenstein,*" *Comparative Literature* 17, No. 2 (1965): p. 100 ff.

51. *The Book of the Thousand Nights and One Night,* trans. John Payne, vol. 2 (London, 1901), pp. 22-25.

52. Sir Richard Burton, trans., *The Arabian Nights* (New York, 1948), p. 154.

53. Louis Awad, "The Alchemist in English Literature. Part I. *Frankenstein.*" Bulletin of the Faculty Arts, Fuad I University, Cairo 13 (May 1951): p. 35.

54. Ibid.

55. Although the Golem is a perennial myth, it is difficult to find reliable sources of information about it. There are extensive and apparently scholarly essays in the *Encyclopaedia Judaica* (New York, 1971), vol. 7, pp. 754-55 and *The Jewish Encyclopedia* (New York, n.d.), pp. 36-37. Both have bibliographies on the subject of articles written in either German or Yiddish. An elaborate compilation and retelling of the myth is Chayim Bloch's *The Golem: Mystical Tales from the Ghetto of Prague* (Blauvelt, N.Y., 1972). Bloch connects the Golem to *Frankenstein,* remarking that the novel of Mary Shelley is a variant form of the Hasidic myth. Hermann Ebeling makes the same connection in his "Die Stunde Frankensteins," *Der Monat,* 19 (March 1967), p. 32. See also Norbert Wiener's *God and Golem, Inc. A Comment on Certain Points where Cybernetics Impinges on Religion* (Cambridge, Mass., 1964), pp. 49, 95. Little scholarly work has been done in this area.

56. Bloch, *The Golem,* p. 34.

57. The various writings attributed to Paracelsus have only recently come under the careful scrutiny of objective scholars. The most scholarly account is Walter Pagel, *Paracelsus: An Introduction to Philosophical Medicine in the Era of the Renaissance* (Basel, 1958). A more general account for the public is Henry M. Pachter, *Magic into Science: The Story of Paracelsus* (New York, 1951). Dr. Pachter's book provides much information about Paracelsus not available elsewhere and is the product of original research, not a compendium of questionable sources. The writings of Paracelsus on occult and scientific matters closely connected with the occult have been largely ignored and are therefore available in only the most questionable forms such as Franz Hartmann's *Paracelsus: His Life and Doctrine* (New York, 1918). Pachter notes that the translations are often very free. In order to discuss the homunculus I am forced to use Hartmann.

58. Hartmann, *Paracelsus,* pp. 32-33.

59. Ibid. Pachter quotes this passage directly from Hartmann because it is the only known translation of the recipe.

60. Ibid., pp. 304-5.

61. Alfred Chapuis and Edmond Droz, *Les automates: figures artificielles d'hommes et d'animaux—histoire et technique* (Neuchatel, Switzerland, n.d.). An elaborate, heavily illustrated, exhaustive treatment of the subject.

62. Paul Fleury Mottelay, *Bibliographic History of Electricity and Magnetism* (London, 1922), p. 177. A remarkable source book for information on this subject not available elsewhere. It is an indispensable work on the history of electricity.

63. Desmond King-Hele, *The Essential Writings of Erasmus Darwin* (London, 1968).
64. E. T. A. Hoffmann, *The Best Tales of Hoffmann*, ed. E. F. Bleiler (New York, 1967), pp. 78–79. Hoffmann's works are difficult to obtain in an English translation. One finds scattered stories in anthologies of the fairy tale but often these are severely cut and revised for the small child. But Hoffmann did not write exclusively for the child as any reading of his rather complicated stories will quickly show. E. F. Bleiler is one of the best known authorities on the fantasy story and his selection in the Dover Press edition of Hoffmann is generous and wide ranging.
65. Ibid., p. 205.
66. It is worth noting that not one speaker in the novel who has the opportunity to observe the artificial man move is struck with any artificiality about it. See for example Victor's description of the Being as it approaches him across the glacial ice of Montanvert.

Notes for Chapter 5

1. Eino Railo, *The Haunted Castle* (New York, 1923), p. 309.
2. Masao Miyoshi, *The Divided Self: A Perspective on the Literature of the Victorians* (New York, 1969), p. 81.
3. For a thorough, general summary of magic, its aims and theory see Manly P. Hall, *An Encyclopedic Outline of Masonic, Hermetic, Qabbalistic and Rosicrucian Symbolical Philosophy* (Los Angeles, 1971), p. 150 ff.
4. Arthur Edward Waite, *The Book of Ceremonial Magic* (New Hyde Park, N.Y., 1916), p. 3 ff. The chapter entitled "The Antiquity of Magical Rituals" discusses the difficulty of acquiring reliable texts of necromantic rituals. Waite's book reprints in a convenient form all the important necromantic sources which are otherwise unobtainable.
5. See Waite's article on "Composite Rituals" in *The Book of Ceremonial Magic* for a discussion of the difficulty that lies in wait for the apprentice magician, p. 58 ff.
6. Shelley, *The 1818 Text*, p. 34.
7. Hall, *Encyclopedic Outline*, p. 150.
8. Ibid. "It is possible to make contracts with spirits whereby the magician becomes for a stipulated time the master of an elemental being."
9. Shelley, *The 1818 Text*, p. 32.
10. Ibid., p. 34.
11. Waite, *Ceremonial Magic*, p. xxviii.
12. Shelley, *The 1818 Text*, p. 228.
13. Ibid., p. 47.
14. Ibid.
15. Ibid., p. 51.
16. Ibid., p. 52.

Notes for Chapter 5

17. Ibid., p. 46.
18. Ibid., pp. 96, 141, 194.
19. Ibid., p. 87.
20. Ibid., p. 199.
21. Ibid., pp. 199–200.
22. For a comprehensive review of Agrippa's *De Occulta Philosophia* see Frances Yates's study "Cornelius Agrippa's Survey of Renaissance Magic" in her *Giordano Bruno and the Hermetic Tradition* (New York, 1969), pp. 130–43.
23. Shelley, *The 1818 Text*, p. 200.
24. Ibid., p. 201.
25. Exodus 22:18.
26. For lists and discussions of materials needed by the magician see Waite, *Ceremonial Magic*, passim.
27. John Read, *Prelude to Chemistry: An Outline of Alchemy, Its Literature and Relationships* (New York, 1937), p. 24. This book is one of several detailed discussions on the subject of alchemy.
28. Allen G. Debus, *The Chemical Dream of the Renaissance* (Cambridge, 1968), p. 7.
29. Allen G. Debus and Robert P. Multhauf, *Alchemy in the Seventeenth Century* (Los Angeles, 1966), p. 94. This book consists of two separate papers read at a Clark Library Seminar, March 12, 1966 at the William Andrews Clark Memorial Library.
30. Donald M. Hassler, *The Comedian as the Letter D: Erasmus Darwin's Comic Materialism* (The Hague, 1973), p. 11. Chapter one of this book is a study of the clash of Newtonian skepticism with religious faith.
31. For another discussion of the clash of ancient authority with skepticism see Charles G. Nauert, Jr., "Magic and Skepticism in Agrippa's Thought," *Journal of the History of Ideas* 18, No. 2 (1957), pp. 160–82.
32. "The Paracelsian physician to the King of Denmark, Peter Severinus, wrote in 1571 that honest students of nature should sell their possessions and burn their books. With the proceeds they must buy sturdy clothes and set out to examine and observe everything with their own eyes. Above all, they should purchase coal, 'build furnaces, watch and operate with the fire without wearying. In this way and no other you will arrive at a knowledge of things and their properties.' " Debus, *The Chemical Dream of the Renaissance*, p. 11.
33. Hartmann has remarked that only those who were diligent and faithful would be able to discover the truth, p. 302n and pp. 305–6.
34. For a description of the closed universe system of the Renaissance, see Yates, *Giordano Bruno*, pp. 144–56.
35. Hall, *Encyclopedic Outline*, p. 149 There is no really satisfactory exposition of the secret doctrine. Its essence lies in its sublime inability to be communicated into words. Its truth lies within the mind of the alchemist, rather than in the exterior world. See also Hartmann's essay of "Alchemy and Astrology" in his *Paracelsus*.

36. Philip P. Wiener, ed., "Alchemy," in *The Dictionary of the History of Ideas*, 4 vols. (New York, 1973), p. 29.
37. Shelley, *The 1818 Text*, p. 34.
38. Read, *Prelude to Chemistry*, p. 118. Of the various discussions of alchemy, Read's book provides the most extensive discussion of the philosopher's stone and the elixir of life.
39. Debus, *Alchemy and Chemistry in the Seventeenth Century*, p. 6.
40. Shelley, *The 1818 Text*, p. 34.
41. Read, *Prelude to Chemistry*, p. 121.
42. Shelley, *The 1818 Text*, p. 35.
43. Ibid., p. 41.
44. Ibid., p. 25.
45. Ibid., p. 45.
46. Ibid., p. 143.
47. L. J. Swingle, "Frankenstein's Monster and Its Romantic Relatives: Problems of Knowledge in English Romanticism," *Texas Studies in Literature and Language: A Journal of the Humanities* 15, No. 1 (Spring 1973).
48. Shelley, *The 1818 Text*, p. 143.

Notes for Chapter 6

1. J. E. McGuire, "Boyles's Conception of Nature," *Journal of the History of Ideas* 33, No. 4 (1972): p. 523. "The 'new science' conceives nature dynamically in terms of motion, rather than statically in terms solely of the size and shape of internal particles; that occult qualities are to be banished from explanations which must be based on sensory experience in terms of clear and distinct ideas; or that nature is to be conceived in analogy to the operations of mechanical activities."
2. Sir Isaac Newton, *Principia Mathematica*, ed. F. Cajori, p. 547. Quoted in "Newton and the Method of Analysis," *Dictionary of the History of Ideas*, p. 378.
3. For a typical exposition of this method at its most extensive, see Herbert Silberer, *Hidden Symbolism of Alchemy and the Occult Arts* (New York, 1971). This is a book-length interpretation of a mystic parable in alchemic and magical terms.
4. H. S. Thayer, ed., *Newton's Philosophy of Nature* (New York, 1953), p. 7. This book presents a generous selection of Newton's ideas in excerpts from key works.
5. John Davy, ed., *The Collected Works of Sir Humphry Davy*, vol. 4 (London, 1840), p. 2.
6. Norman L. Torrey, ed., *Les Philosophes* (New York, 1960), p. 201. This useful book gathers representative writings of the French Enlightenment together in one volume.
7. R. W. Harris, *Reason and Nature in the Eighteenth Century* (New York, 1969), p. 10. Of this revolutionary position Harris remarks that "the seventeenth-century scientists dealt classical humanism a series of shattering blows . . . it seemed clear that there

was a physical world governed by laws ascertainable by the human mind. These laws were to be discovered, not by *a priori* reasoning, not by some reference to an authority, such as the ancient philosophers, or the Scriptures, but by empirical means."

8. E. W. Strong, "Newtonian Explications of Natural Philosophy," *Journal of the History of Ideas* 18, No. 1 (1957), p. 49. This was the Cartesian dilemma. Pure thought alone was proving incapable of uncovering the underlying truth of the universe. "Newton asserts that we cannot 'certainly determine' from mental conceivability and mathematical demonstration that parts are actually divided and separated 'to infinity' by the powers of Nature." The only way we can know about the "qualities of bodies" is through experiment.

9. Davy, *The Collected Works*, p. 3.

10. Gerald R. Cragg, *Reason and Authority in the Eighteenth Century* (Cambridge, 1964), p. 2. "Thus all forms of traditional authority were suspect. In both moral and the political spheres the new age subtly shifted the grounds of confidence. Nothing was to be taken on trust. Men were to be taught to rely on the evidence provided by nature or reason, not on the arguments supplied by tradition."

11. Shelley, *The 1818 Text*, p. 34.

12. Ibid.

13. Ibid., p. 35.

14. Ibid.

15. Joseph Priestley, *The History of the Present State of Electricity with Original Experiments*, introd. Robert E. Schofield, 3rd ed., The Sources of Science, No. 18 (New York, 1966), 2, p. 204 ff.

16. Ibid., p. 204.

17. Shelley, *The 1818 Text*, p. 35.

18. Priestley, *State of Electricity*, p. 106 ff.

19. Ibid., II, p. 107.

20. Ibid., pp. 107–8.

21. In addition to Schofield's study of this subject in his *Mechanism and Materialism: British Natural Philosophy in an Age of Reason* (Princeton, 1970), see also Arnold Thackray, *Atoms and Powers: An Essay On Newtonian Matter—Theory and the Development of Chemistry* (Harvard, 1970). For a discussion of the two books, their similarities and differences, see the thorough review of Thackray's book in the *Philological Quarterly* 50, No. 3 (July 1972), by John R. R. Christie.

22. Radu Florescu, *In Search of Frankenstein* (Boston, 1975), p. 173.

23. Shelley, *The 1818 Text*, p. 40.

24. Ibid., p. 41.

25. Only in recent years have important early researchers such as Paracelsus been relieved of the opprobrium with which they have been traditionally assigned. For an enlightened and illuminating assessment of Paracelsus's true value in the history of

science, see Walter Pagel, *Paracelsus: An Introduction to Philosophical Medicine in the Era of the Renaissance* (Basel, 1958).

26. Shelley, *The 1818 Text*, p. 42.

27. L. J. Swingle, "Frankenstein's Monster and Its Romantic Relatives: Problems of Knowledge in English Romanticism," *Texas Studies in Literature and Language: A Journal of the Humanities*, 15, No. 1 (Spring 1973). Swingle is the first critic to cast doubt on Victor as Mary's spokesman in the novel.

28. Ibid., p. 60.

29. Shelby T. McCloy, *French Inventions of the Eighteenth Century* (Lexington, Ken., 1952), p. 149. McCloy's book is particularly helpful because of the extensive bibliographies he includes under his subject headings.

30. For a brief survey of Malpighi's contributions see Dampier, *A History of Science and Its Relations with Philosophy and Religion* (Cambridge, 1961), p. 120 ff.

31. Shelley, *The 1818 Text*, p. 42.

32. Dampier, *A History of Science*, p. 120.

33. For my knowledge of early airships I have relied on A. Wolf, *A History of Science, Technology, and Philosophy in the 18th Century* (New York, 1961), p. 577 ff.

34. In addition to Wolf's review of this subject in volume one of the above work, see J. R. Partington, *A Short History of Chemistry* (New York, 1965) for a lengthy and penetrating summary.

35. A contemporary account of the composition of the atmosphere can be found in Davy's *Elements of Chemistry*, pp. 165–235.

36. Ibid., p. 18.

37. Shelley, *The 1818 Text*, p. 42.

38. A contemporary account calls the magic lantern "a very remarkable machine, which is now known over all the world, [and] caused great astonishment at its origin." W. Hooper, *Rational Recreations, in Which the Principles of Numbers and Natural Philosophy are Clearly and Copiously Elucidated*, etc. (London, 1782), 2nd ed., p. 32. For a lengthy history and treatise on the subject consult Henry Simon Gage, *Optic Projections* (New York, 1914).

39. I hesitate to introduce a popular book in a discussion of magic lanterns, but material discussing the invention is difficult to find. Peter Haining has recently published a pictorial history of the subject of ghosts in which he discusses the early deceptions which were made possible by use of the magic lantern or phantasmagoria. *Ghosts* (New York, 1976), pp. 60–61.

40. Haining, *Ghosts*, p. 160. Haining reprints a number of rare prints of Robertson's theater and its method of operation.

41. Hooper, *Rational Recreations*, p. 32 ff.

42. Ibid., pp. 44–47; Haining, *Ghosts*, p. 160.

43. Haining, *Ghosts*, Plate 3, vol. 2.

Notes for Chapter 6

44. Hooper, *Rational Recreations*, p. 46.
45. Haining's book reproduces a rare, contemporary print showing this very experiment in operation, p. 160.
46. Hooper, *Rational Recreations*, p. 47.
47. Charles Hutton, trans., *Recreations in Science and Natural Philosophy,* revis. Edward Riddle (London, 1844), p. 324 ff. In 1803 Dr. Charles Hutton translated into English a French work on science in which detailed drawings and explanations of the solar microscope were printed.
48. Hutton, *Recreations in Science,* p. 324.
49. Ibid.
50. The part of the manuscript now extant is the section of the novel dealing with Victor's education at Ingolstadt. The writing flows down the page with few corrections.
51. *Edinburgh Review* 39 (October 1809), p. 53 ff.
52. Ibid., p. 71.
53. See the chapter entitled "Interest in the Occult at German Universities," in Lynn Thorndike's *History of Magic and Experimental Science* (New York, 1958), pp. 339–71.
54. Ibid., p. 340.
55. Ibid., p. 341.
56. Shelley, *The 1818 Text,* pp. 40–41.
57. For Mary's personal remarks (and they are very few in number) about her perusal of Davy see *Mary Shelley's Journals,* ed. Frederick L. Jones (Norman, Okla., 1947). Mary first mentions reading Davy on October 28, 1816 and mentions his name in her journal for several days thereafter.
58. Davy, *The Collected Works,* p. 1.
59. Shelley, *The 1818 Text,* p. 46.
60. Davy, *The Collected Works,* p. 43. S. E. Toulmin provides a good insight as to why Mary should depict Victor examining the decay of human flesh while searching for what is essentially a chemical answer. Toulmin points out "there was great obscurity about the distinction between chemical processes and physical ones: the more often light, for instance, was thought of as a substance, the more tendency was there to treat optical phenomena as effects of combination and decomposition." "Crucial Experiments: Priestley, Lavoisier," *Journal of the History of Ideas* 18 (April 1957), p. 215.
61. George Sarton discusses this obstacle in his article "The New Anatomy" in *Six Wings: Men of Science in the Renaissance* (New York, 1957), p. 172 ff.
62. Ibid., p. 173.
63. Charles Dickens's novel was a highly accurate portrayal of revolutionary France written after Dickens had engaged in much research on the subject. Consult Albert C. Baugh, *A Literary History of England* (New York, 1967), p. 1350.

64. Xavier Bichat, *Physiological Researches upon Life and Death* (Philadelphia, 1809), p. 275.

65. Regardless of the purpose, such an experience would be difficult even for the most devoted student of science or art. Leonardo de Vinci was forced into a similar situation when he wanted to draw the anatomy of the human body but was forbidden to dissect a corpse. He says, "Though possessed of an interest in the subject you may perhaps be deterred by natural repugnance, or, if this does not restrain you, then perhaps by the fear of passing the night hours in the company of these corpses, quartered and flayed and horrible to behold. . . ." Quoted by Gillespie in *The Edge of Objectivity* (Princeton, 1960), p. 56. I assume the translation is Gillespie's.

66. Shelley, *The 1818 Text*, p. 47.

67. James Boswell, "An Account of My Last Interview with David Hume, Esq.," *Private Papers of James Boswell,* ed. Geoffrey Scott and Frederick A. Pottle (Mount Vernon, Va., 1931), pp. 227–32. Of interest in this connection is James Boswell's death-bed interview with David Hume. Boswell had the tasteless effrontery to inquire if Hume, now that he was dying, had changed his mind. He was told that Hume had not. This article is conveniently reprinted in Hume's *Dialogues Concerning Natural Religion*, ed. Norman Kemp Smith (New York, 1947), pp. 76–79.

68. William Hazlitt, *An Essay on the Principles of Human Action and Some Remarks on the Systems of Hartley and Helvetius,* introd. John R. Nabholtz, a facsimile reproduction (Gainesville, Fl., 1969). Detachment is the hallmark of the materialist and is one of the factors that so disturbed those who were not able to practice it. See for example Hazlitt's trouble in accepting Hartley's materialism. Hazlitt remarks, "I think Hartley constantly mistakes tracing the order of palpable effects, or overt acts of the mind for explaining the causes of the connection between them, which he hardly ever does with true metaphysical feeling. Even where he is greatest, *he is always the physiologist rather than the metaphysician*" [emphasis mine].

69. Sir Humphry Davy, *Works: Agricultural Lectures, Part II and Other Lectures,* 8, p. 167.

70. Shelley, *The 1818 Text,* p. 47.

71. Davy, *Works,* 8, p. 167.

72. Shelley, *The 1818 Text,* p. 47.

73. Davy, *Works,* 8, p. 288.

74. Even Lavoisier understood that there was terrible confusion. "Lavoisier remembered with impatience the confusion that had presided over his own chemical education: the preliminary Newtonian pieties in no way borne out by the chaos of ingredients and recipes, the contrast between these verbal thickets and courses on mathematics wherein consequences really did open out of postulates and definitions, the professor's tacitly sharing his bewilderment by supposing that his pupils already knew what he was unsure how to teach" (Gillespie, p. 203).

75. Toulmin, "Crucial Experiments," p. 214.

76. Aram Vartanian, "Trembley's Polyp, La Mettrie, and Eighteenth-Century French Materialism," *JHI* 11, No. 3 (June 1950), p. 272.

77. Shelley, *The 1818 Text,* p. 47.

Notes for Chapter 6

78. One of Schofield's major contributions to the history of materialism is his presentation of the wide variety of thought that all comes under the heading of Newtonianism.
79. Thackray, *Atoms and Powers,* p. 2.
80. "The degree to which Shelley was a scientist in the modern meaning of the term is difficult to decide. His actual experimentation seems to have been restricted to his earlier years before he devoted himself to reform and to have been limited to chemistry and electricity. But he evidently continued to be widely read in scientific philosophy and to the last found in it a suggestion and inspiration for poetry." Grabo, *A Newton Among Poets,* pp. 35–36. See also Rieger's assessment of Shelley as a scientist in his introduction to *Frankenstein..*
81. James Rieger, "Dr. Polidori and the Genesis of *Frankenstein,*" *Studies in English Literature* 3, No. 4 (Autumn 1963), p. 468.
82. Shelley, *The 1818 Text,* p. 10. One of the things Walton hopes to clear up is the mystery of the aurora borealis. For a lengthy discussion on this subject see the essay by J. Morton Briggs, Jr., "Aurora and Enlightenment: Eighteenth-Century Explanations of the Aurora Borealis," *Isis* 58, Part 4, No. 194 (1967), pp. 491–503.
83. Shelley, *The 1818 Text,* p. 11.
84. Harris, *Reason and Nature,* p. 10.
85. Bichat's work, for example, was all done by direct observation and dissection of cadavers, both animal and human.
86. For summaries of scientists and their accomplishments, see René Taton, *History of Science: the Beginnings of Modern Science: 1480–1800,* trans. A. J. Pomerans (New York, 1964), vol. 7.
87. Walter D. Wetzels, "Aspects of Natural Science in German Romanticism," *Studies in Romanticism* 10, No. 1 (Winter 1971), p. 52. Although *Naturphilosophie* was eventually discredited, it enjoyed a great vogue.
88. Shelley, *The 1818 Text,* p. 6.
89. "Not thus, after all, would life be given. Perhaps a corpse would be re-animated; galvanism had given token of such things. . . ." (p. 227).
90. Wetzels, "Aspects of Natural Science," p. 52.
91. Ibid. For other experiments of Ritter with galvanism, read Barry Gower, "Speculation in Physics: the History and Practice of *Naturphilosophe,*" *Studies in the History and Philosophy of Science* 3, No. 4 (1973), pp. 301–56.
92. Paul Mottelay, *Bibliographic History of Electricity and Magnetism* (London, 1922), pp. 304–6.
93. Ibid., p. 305.
94. Ibid., p. 304.
95. Ibid. Mottelay's bibliography shows that Aldini's experiments were published in at least twenty-five books and periodicals before 1816.
96. "An account of the late Improvements in Galvanism, with a Series of Curious and Interesting Experiments, performed before the Commissioners of the French Na-

tional Institute, and repeated lately in the Anatomical Theatres of London, by John Aldini, Professor of Experimental Philosophy in the University of Bologna," *Edinburgh Review* 3 (October 1803), pp. 194–98.

97. Ibid., p. 196.
98. Ibid., p. 197.
99. Mottelay, *Bibliographic History,* p. 375.
100. Ibid.
101. Ibid., p. 305.
102. Shelley, *The 1818 Text,* p. 49.
103. Ibid., p. 52.
104. Mary is, perhaps of necessity, reticent about the implements used by Victor in his animation of the artificial man. We do know that when Victor began to create the artificial female in the Scottish islands, he used chemical instruments although they are not described. We are told that he packed his "chemical instruments" and we are also given a picture of Victor "upon the beach, employed in cleaning and arranging [his] chemical apparatus" (*Frankenstein,* pp. 167–68).
105. Bichat is not the only researcher who went about extraordinary research in a detached manner. See Galvani's letter to Professor Don Bassano Carminati in which he discusses his recent electrical experiments on the freshly amputated leg of a patient in the Hospital of Saint Ursula. Galvani does not tell us whether he received permission from the patient but he leaves a clear record of the experiment in which he was able to attach an armature of tin-foil to the raw stump which had been "denuded of their integuments" (*De Viribus Electricitatus,* p. 97).
106. Bichat, *Physiological Researches,* p. 275.
107. Ibid.
108. Rieger has shown that Mary's memory of these events is often faulty. There is no record of them in her letters or her journal.
109. Rieger, "Dr. Polidori", pp. 468–69.
110. I have been unable to uncover research which would help establish this point.
111. McCloy, *French Inventions,* pp. 148–69.
112. Ibid., pp. 162–63.
113. For a full account of this examine the *Mémoires de Madame la Comtesse de Genlis, sur le dix-huitième siècle et la Révolution française, depuis 1756 jusqu'à nos jours,* 2nd. ed. (Paris, 1825), vol. 1, pp. 338–39.
114. Ibid., p. 338.
115. McCloy, *French Inventions,* p. 163.
116. Burton R. Pollin, "Philosophical and Literary Sources of *Frankenstein,*" *Comparative Literature,* 17, pp. 100–101.
117. Brian Aldiss, *The Billion Year Spree* (New York, 1973), p. 21.

Bibliography

Aldini, John. "An account of the late Improvements in Galvanism, with a Series of Curious and Interesting Experiments performed before the Commissioners of the French National Institute, and repeated lately in the Anatomical Theatres of London." *Edinburgh Review* 3 (1803): 194–98.
Aldiss, Brian. *The Billion Year Spree.* New York, 1970.
Awad, Louis. "The Alchemist in English Literature. Part I. *Frankenstein.*" *Bulletin of the Faculty Arts, Fuad I University, Cairo* 13 (1951): 33–82.
Baugh, Albert C. *A Literary History of England.* New York, 1967.
Beckford, William. *Vathek.* Translated by Herbert B. Grimsditch. London, 1948.
Bichat, Xavier. *Physiological Researches on Life and Death.* 1st American from the 2nd Paris ed. Philadelphia, 1809.
Biglund, Eileen. *Mary Shelley.* London, 1959.
Birkhead, Edith. *The Tale of Terror: A Study of the Gothic Romance.* London, 1921.
Bloch, Chayim. *The Golem: Mystical Tales from the Ghetto of Prague.* Blauvelt, N.Y., 1972.
Bloom, Harold. "Frankenstein, or the New Prometheus." *Partisan Review* 32 (1965): 611–18.
Boswell, James. *Private Papers of James Boswell.* Edited by Geoffrey Scott and Frederick A. Pottle. Mount Vernon, Va., 1931.
Boyd, John D. *The Function of Mimesis and Its Decline.* Harvard, 1968.
Briggs, J. Morton, Jr. "Aurora and Enlightenment: Eighteenth-Century Explanations of the Aurora Borealis." *Isis* 58 (1967): No. 194.
Burton, Sir Richard. *The Arabian Nights.* New York, 1948.
Callaghan, Cecily. "Mary Shelley's *Frankenstein*: A Compendium of Romanticism." Unpublished dissertation, Leland Stanford Junior University, 1936.
Callahan, Patrick J. "Frankenstein, Bacon, and the Two Truths." *Extrapolation* 14 (1972): No. 1.
Campbell, Blair. "La Mettrie: The Robot and the Automaton." *Journal of the History of Ideas* 31 (1970): 555–72.
Chapuis, Alfred and Edmond Droz. *Les automates: figures artificielles d'hommes et d'animaux—histoire et technique.* Neuchatel, Switzerland, n.d.
Christie, John R. R. "Review of Thackray's *Atoms and Powers.*" *Philolological Quarterly* 50 (1972): No. 3.
Church, Richard. *Mary Shelley.* New York, 1928.
Condillac, Etienne de Bonnot. *Treatise on the Sensations.* Translated by Geraldine Carr. Los Angeles, 1930.
Conklin, E. G. "Joseph Priestley and the American Philosophic Society: His Experiments on Spontaneous Generation." *Proceedings of the American Philosophical Society* 59 (1950): No. 2.

Crafts, Stephen. "*Frankenstein:* Camp Curiosity or Premonition." *Catalyst* 3 (1971): 96–103.
Cragg, Gerald R. *Reason and Authority in the Eighteenth Century.* Cambridge, 1964.
Crombie, A. C. *Medieval and Early Modern Science.* 2 vols. New York, 1959.
Dampier, Sir William Cecil. *A History of Science and its Relations with Philosophy and Religion.* Postscript by Bernard Cohen. Cambridge, 1961.
Davy, Sir Humphry. *The Collected Works of Sir Humphry Davy.* 8 vols. London, 1840.
Debus, Allen G. and Multhauf, Robert. *Alchemy in the Seventeenth Century.* Los Angeles, 1966.
Debus, Allen G. *The Chemical Dream of the Renaissance.* Cambridge, 1968.
de Genlis, Comptesse. *Mémoires de Madame la Comptesse de Genlis, sur le dix-huitième siècle et la Révolution française, depuis 1756 jusqu'à nos jours.* 2 vols. 2nd. ed. Paris, 1825.
Dickens, Charles. *A Tale of Two Cities.* New York, 1966.
"Discours sur les Progrès des Sciences, Lettres et Arts, depuis 1789 jusqu'à ce jour (1808); ou, Compte rendu par l'Institut de France a S. M. l'Empereur et Roi." *Edinburgh Review* 29 (1809): 1–53.
Ebeling, Hermann. "Die Stunde Frankensteins." *Der Monat* 19 (March 1967).
Edinburgh Review 39 (October 1809).
Fleck, P. D. "Mary Shelley's Notes to Shelley's Poems and *Frankenstein.*" *Studies in Romanticism* 6 (1967): 226–54.
Florescu, Radu. *In Search of* Frankenstein. Boston, 1975.
Gage, Henry Simon. *Optic Projections.* New York, 1914.
Galvani, Luigi. *De Viribus Electricitatus in Motor Musculari Commentarius.* Translated by Robert Montraveille Green. Cambridge, Mass., 1953.
Gay, Peter. *The Enlightenment: An Interpretation.* 2 vols. New York, 1969.
Gerson, Noel Bertram. *Daughter of Earth and Water.* New York, 1973.
Gillespie, Charles Coulston. *The Edge of Objectivity.* Princeton, 1960.
"The Golem." *Encyclopaedia Judaica.* New York, 1971. Also *The Jewish Encyclopedia.* New York, n.d.
Goldberg, M. A. "Moral and Myth in Mrs. Shelley's *Frankenstein.*" *Keats-Shelley Journal* 8 (1959): 27–38.
Gower, Barry. "Speculation in Physics: The History and Practice of *Naturphilosophie.*" *Studies in the History and Philosophy of Science* 3 (1973): 301–56.
Grabo, Carl. *A Newton Among Poets.* New York, 1968.
──────. *Prometheus Unbound: An Interpretation.* Chapel Hill, N.C., 1935.
Grylls, R. Glynn. *Mary Shelley: A Biography.* London, 1938.
Haining, Peter. *Ghosts: A Pictorial History.* New York, 1976.
Hall, Manly Palmer. *An Encyclopedic Outline of Masonic, Hermetic, Qabbalistic and Rosicrucian Symbolical Philosophy.* Los Angeles, 1971.
Harris, R. W. *Reason and Nature in the Eighteenth Century.* New York, 1969.
Hartley, David. *Observations on Man, His Frame, His Duty, and His Expectations.* A facsimile reproduction of the 1749 ed. 2 vols. in one. Gainesville, Fl., 1966.
Hartmann, Franz. *Paracelsus: His Life and Doctrine.* New York, 1918.
Hassler, Donald M. *The Comedian as the Letter D: Erasmus Darwin's Comic Materialism.* The Hague, 1973.
Hazlitt, William. *An Essay on the Principles of Human Action and Some Remarks on the Systems of Hartley and Helvetius.* A facsimile reproduction with an introduction by John R. Nabholtz. Gainesville, Fl., 1969.
Hoffmann, E. T. A. *The Best Tales of Hoffmann.* Edited by E. F. Bleiler. New York, 1967.

Hogg, Thomas Jefferson. *The Life of Percy Bysshe Shelley*. Introduction by Edward Dowden. New York, 1906.
Homer. *The Iliad*. Introduction by Gilbert Highet. New York, 1950.
Hooper, W. *Rational Recreations, in Which the Principles of Numbers and Natural Philosophy are Clearly and Copiously Elucidated, by a Series of Easy, Entertaining, Interesting Experiments*, etc. 4 vols. 2nd ed. London, 1782.
Hume, David. *Dialogues Concerning Natural Religion*. Edited by Norman Kemp Smith. New York, 1947.
Hutton, Dr. Charles, trans. *Recreations in Science and Natural Philosophy*. Revis. Edward Riddle. London, 1844.
Jones, Frederick L., ed. *Mary Shelley's Journals*. Norman, Okla., 1947.
Kiely, Robert. *The Romantic Novel in England*. Harvard, 1972.
King-Hele, Desmond. *The Essential Writings of Erasmus Darwin*. London, 1968.
La Mettrie, Julien Offroy de. *Man a Machine*. Translated by Gertrude Carman Bussey, et al. La Salle, Ill., 1912.
Lund, Mary Graham. "Mary Godwin Shelley and the Monster." *University of Kansas City Review* 28 (1962): 253-58.
_____. "Shelley as Frankenstein." *Forum* 4 (Fall 1963).
Lyon, G. F. *The Private Journal of G. G. Lyon of H. M. S. Hecla*. London, 1824. Reprinted by the Imprint Society. Barre, Mass., 1970.
Marshall, Mrs. Julian. *The Life and Letters of Mary Wollstonecraft Shelley*. 2 vols. London, 1889.
Mays, Milton. "*Frankenstein,* Mary Shelley's Black Theodicy." *Southern Humanities Review* 3 (1969): No. 2, 1969.
McCloy, Shelby T. *French Inventions of the Eighteenth Century*. Lexington, Ken., 1952.
McGuire, J. E. "Boyles's Conception of Nature." *Journal of the History of Ideas* 33, No. 4 (October 1972).
Millhauser, Milton, "The Noble Savage in *Frankenstein*." *Notes and Queries* 190 (1946): 248-50.
Miyoshi, Masao. *The Divided Self: A Perspective on the Literature of the Victorians*. New York, 1964.
Mottelay, Paul Fleury. *Bibliographic History of Electricity and Magnetism*. London, 1922.
Moore, Helen. *Mary Wollstonecraft Shelley*. Philadelphia, 1886.
Nauert, Charles G. Jr. "Magic and Skepticism in Agrippa's Thought." *Journal of the History of Ideas* 18 (1957): 160-82.
Nelson, Lowry. "Night Thoughts on the Gothic Novel." *Yale Review* 52 (December 1962).
Nitchie, Elizabeth. *Mary Shelley*. New Brunswick, N.J., 1953.
Norman, Sylva. "Mary Wollstonecraft Shelley." In *Shelley and His Circle*. Edited by Kenneth Neill Cameron. 12 vols. Cambridge, Mass., 1970.
Ozolins, Aija. "The Novels of Mary Shelley: From *Frankenstein* to *Falkner*." Unpublished dissertation, University of Maryland, 1972.
Pachter, Henry M. *Magic into Science: The Story of Paracelsus*. New York, 1951.
Pagel, Walter. *Paracelsus: An Introduction to Philosophical Medicine in the Era of the Renaissance*. Basel, 1958.
Partington, J. R. *A Short History of Chemistry*. New York, 1965.
Payne, John, trans. *The Book of the Thousand Nights and One Night*. 9 vols. London, 1901.
Pollin, Burton R. "Philosophical and Literary Sources of *Frankenstein*." *Comparative Literature* 17:97-108.
Priestley, Joseph. *The History of the Present State of Electricity with Original Experiments*.

2 vols. 3rd ed. 1755. A facsimile ed. Introduction by Robert E. Schofield. New York, 1966.

Railo, Eino. *The Haunted Castle: A Study of the Elements of English Romanticism*. New York, 1927.

Rao, E. Nageswara."The Significance of *Frankenstein*." *Triveni* 37 (October 1968).

Read, John. *Prelude to Chemistry: An Outline of Alchemy, Its Literature and Relationships*. New York, 1937.

Reiman, Donald H., ed. *The Romantics Reviewed*. 3 vols. in 9. New York, 1972.

"Review of *Frankenstein*." *The Quarterly Review* 18 (January 1818).

Rieger, James. "Dr. Polidori and the Genesis of *Frankenstein*." *Studies in English Literature* 3 (1963): No. 4.

Rosenfeld, L. "Condillac's Influence on French Scientific Thought." *The Triumph of Culture: 18th Century Perspectives*. Edited by Paul Fritz and David Williams. Toronto, 1972.

Rossetti, Lucy Maddox. *Mrs. Shelley*. London, 1890.

Sarton, George. *Six Wings: Men of Science in the Renaissance*. New York, 1957.

Schofield, Robert. *Mechanism and Materialism: British Natural Philosophy in an Age of Reason*. Princeton, 1970.

──────. *A Scientific Autobiography of Joseph Priestley, 1733–1804*. Cambridge, Mass., 1966.

Scott, Sir Walter. *Critical and Miscellaneous Essays of Sir Walter Scott, Collected by Himself*. 2 vols. Philadelphia, 1841.

Shelley, Mary. *Frankenstein*. Bodleian MS. Abinger 63.

──────. *Frankenstein*. Edited by R. E. Douse and D. J. Palmer. London, 1963.

──────. *Frankenstein*. MS. microfilm collection. Duke University. Reels 6 and 11.

──────. *Frankenstein*. Ed. M. K. Joseph. Oxford, 1971.

──────. *Frankenstein, the 1818 Text*. Edited by James Rieger. Indianapolis, 1974.

──────. *Tales and Stories*. Ed. Richard Garnett. London, 1891.

Shelley, Percy Bysshe. *The Poems of Shelley*. London, n.d.

Shugg, Wallace. "The Cartesian Beast-Machine in English Literature (1661–1750)." *Journal of the History of Ideas* 29 (1968): No. 2.

Silberer, Herbert. *Hidden Symbolism of Alchemy and the Occult Arts*. New York, 1971.

Small, Christopher. *Mary Shelley's Frankenstein: Tracing the Myth*. Pittsburgh, 1972.

Spark, Muriel. "Mary Shelley: A Prophetic Novelist." *The Listener* 22 (February 1951): 205–6.

Strong, E. W. "Newtonian Explications of Natural Philosophy." *Journal of the History of Ideas* 18 (1957): No. 1.

Swingle, L. J. "Frankenstein's Monster and Its Romantic Relatives: Problems of Knowledge in English Romanticism." *Texas Studies in Literature and Language: A Journal of the Humanities* 15 (1973): No. 1.

Taton René. *History of Science. The Beginnings of Modern Science: 1480–1800*. Translated by A. J. Pomerans. Vol. 7. New York, 1964.

Thackray, Arnold. *Atoms and Powers: An Essay on Newtonian Matter—Theory and the Development of Chemistry*. Harvard, 1970.

Thayer, H. S., ed. *Newton's Philosophy of Nature*. New York, 1953.

Thorndike, Lynn. *History of Magic and Experimental Science*. 1923. 8 vols. Reprint. New York, 1958.

Torrey, Norman L. *Les Philosophes*. New York, 1960.

Toulmin, S. E. "Crucial Experiments: Priestley and Lavoisier." *Journal of the History of Ideas* 18 (April 1957).

Trawick, Leonard, ed. *Backgrounds of Romanticism: English Philosophical Prose of the Eighteenth Century.* Bloomington, 1967.
Tropp, Martin. "Mary Shelley's Monster: A Study of *Frankenstein.*" Unpublished dissertation, Boston University, 1973.
Vartanian, Aram. "Trembley's Polyp, La Mettrie, and Eighteenth-Century French Materialism." *Journal of the History of Ideas* 11 (1950): 272.
"A View of Spain; Comprising a Descriptive Itinerary of each Province, and a General Statistical Account of the Country." *Edinburgh Review* 29 (1809): 53–72.
Vlasopolos, Anca. "*Frankenstein's* Hidden Skeleton: The Psycho-Politics of Oppression." *Science-Fiction Studies* 10 (July 1983).
Waite, Arthur Edward. *The Book of Ceremonial Magic: The Secret Tradition in Goëtia, including the Rites and Mysteries of Goëtic Theurgy, Sorcery, and Infernal Necromancy.* New York, 1961.
Walling, William A. *Mary Shelley.* New York, 1972.
Wiener, Norbert. *God and Golem, Inc. A Comment on Certain Points Where Cybernetics Impinges on Religion.* Cambridge, Mass., 1964.
Wiener, Philip P., ed. *The Dictionary of the History of Ideas.* 4 vols. New York, 1973.
Wetzels, Walter D. "Aspects of Natural Science in German Romanticism." *Studies in Romanticism* 10 (1971): No. 11.
White, Newman Ivy. *Shelley.* 2 vols. New York, 1940.
Wolf, A. *A History of Science, Technology, and Philosophy in the 18th Century.* New York, 1961.
Yates, Francis. *Giordano Bruno and the Hermetic Tradition.* New York, 1969.

Index

Abinger collection, 31
Aeschylus
   Prometheus Bound, 21
Agrippa, Henry Cornelius, 1, 25, 29, 68, 69, 74, 81
Agrippan sorcery, 56
airships, 71
Albertus Magnus, 60, 61, 68, 69
alchemy, 1, 13, 29, 47-48, 51-61
   conflict with science, 60
   confusion of magic and chemistry, 58
   defined, 56
   elixir of life, 58-59
   magic compared to, 56-58
   observation of nature, 57
   philosopher's stone, 58-59
   secret doctrine, 58
   universal view, 57
Aldini, Giovanni, 80
   electrification of human corpses, 79-80
Aldiss, Brian
   Billion Year Spree, The, 26
Amis, Kingsley
   New Maps of Hell, 28
animated statue, 45-47
   in antiquity, 45-46
   the Golem, 46
   medieval versions of, 46
artificial man
   animation of, 54
   compared to automata, 49-50
   compared to Golem, 46-47
   compared to homunculus, 48
   compared to statue, 45-46
   construction of, 38-39
   its personality, 36
   physical description, 35ff.
automata, 48-50
   of E. Darwin, 49
   in E.T.A. Hoffmann's *Tales,* 49
   of Wolfgang von Kempelen, 48-49

Awad, Lewis, 13
   alchemy in *Frankenstein,* 13

Bacon, Francis, 25-26
Bacon, Roger (pseudo), 56
Beckford, William
   Vathek, 21
Bichat, Xavier
   morbid anatomy, 70, 75
   Physiological Researches on Life and Death, 39, 81
   Treatise on Membranes, 70
Biglund, Eileen, 14
Biheron, Mademoiselle, 81-82
Birkhead, Edith, 9-11
Blackwood's Edinburgh Magazine, 5-6
Bloom, Harold, 17

Callahan, Patrick J., 25, 30
Carpue, J.C.S.
   electrification of corpse, 80
Chapuis, Alfred
   automata, 48
chemistry, 74, 76-77
Church, Richard, 11-12
Clairmont, Claire
   letters of, 31
Condillac, Etienne Bonnot de, 17, 43-45, 50, 83
   Statue device in *Frankenstein,* 19, 45
   Traité du sensations, 19, 39, 43-45
Cotes, Roger, 65
Crafts, Stephen, 20

Darwin, Erasmus, 2, 27
   speaking head, 48-49
   vermicelli, 79
Davy, Sir Humphry, 2, 76
   Agricultural Lectures, 76
   air pump, 71, 73
   Elements of Chemical Philosophy, 65-66, 74

Index

Diderot, Denis, 17, 19
  Lettre sur les aveugles, 19
  Lettre sur les sourds et muets, 19
  Thoughts on the Interpretation of Nature, 66
Douse, R.E., 16
Droz, Edmond, 48

Edinburgh Magazine, 5-6
electricity, 60, 67-69, 79
elixir of life (Grand Elixir), 59

Fantasmagoriana, 15
Faust, 18, 20, 23
Fleck, P.D., 21-22
Florescu, Radu, 29-30
  alchemy in *Frankenstein*, 30
Frankenstein, or the New Prometheus
  eighteenth-century science, 25, 65ff.
  Gothic elements in, 23, 25
  literary analogues, 17-19, 21-22
  literary sources, 17-19, 22, 29, 30
  manuscript of, 31ff.
  microfilm of, 31
  as moral fable, 14, 16-17, 24
  as myth, 16, 17, 20, 23, 27
  Promethean theme, 14, 25
  sources of novel, 14, 15, 16, 24, 30
  as speculative fiction, 14, 23, 24, 25, 26, 28

Galvani, Luigi, 39
Garnett, Richard, 8-9
Genlis, Mme. de
  Mémoires, 82
Gentleman's Magazine, 6
Gerson, Noel, 24-25
Gisbourne, John
  Journal, 31
Godwin, William, 27, 29
  St. Leon, 21
  Caleb Williams, 21
Goethe, Wolfgang von
  Sorrows of Werther, 21
Goldberg, M.A., 14
Golem, 46-47
Grabo, Carl, 1
Grylls, R. Glynn, 7, 12

Hartley, David
  Observations on Man, His Frame, His Duty, and His Expectations, 39ff., 43
hasidism, 46
Heinlein, Robert A., 2
Hephaestos, 46
Hoffmann, E.T.A.
  "Automata" (story), 49
  "The Sandman" (story), 49

homunculus, 47-48
Hooper, Dr. W.
  Rational Recreations, 72
  magic lantern described by, 72

Ingolstadt, University of, 69
  teaching at, 67, 73-74

Joseph, M.K., 24

Kempelen, Wolfgang von
  speaking machine, 48
Kiely, Robert, 24

La Belle Assemblée, 26
Laurent, Pierre Joseph, 81
Les Portraits de Famille, 15
Lithuania, 44
Locke, John, 24
  Essay Concerning Human Understanding, 17
Lowe, Rabbi, 46-47
Lund, Mary Graham, 16

magic
  in Agrippa, 52
  in Albertus Magnus, 52
  defined, 52
  in *Frankenstein*, 53-56, 73-74
magic lantern, 71, 72
Marshall, Mrs. Julian, 8
Mays, Milton, 23
Mettrie, Julien Offroy de la, 77
  Man a Machine, 40ff.
Millhauser, Prof. Milton, 12
Milton, John
  Paradise Lost, 17, 18, 23
  themes in *Frankenstein*, 18
Miyoshi, Masao, 22-23, 51
Mottelay, Paul Fleury
  Bibliographic History of Electricity and Magnetism, 48, 79
Moore, Helen
  biography of Mary Shelley, 7-8

Naturphilosophie, 78-79
Needham, Joseph, 24
Nelson, Lowry, 14
New Science
  defined, 65
  methods, 65
  operative in *Frankenstein*, 60, 66ff., 71, 74, 78, 83-84
  principles of, 65-66
Newton, Sir Isaac, 65-66
Nitchie, Elizabeth, 13-14
Nollet, Abbé, 68

Norman, Sylva, 23
Nouveaux Nouvelles, 18

Ovid
　Metamorphoses, 18
Ozolins, Aija, 24

Palmer, D.J., 16-17
Paracelsus, 1, 25, 29, 61, 68, 69
　homunculus of, 47-48
philosopher's stone, 59
physiology, 70, 74-75, 78, 82
Polidori, John William
　De Oneirodynia, 15
　the physician, 15
　as source of ideas, 21, 77-78
　The Vampyre, 15
Pollin, Burton R., 17-20, 30
Priestley, Joseph, 2, 39
　History of Electricity, 39, 67-68
Prometheus, 17, 21
Ptah, 46, 47
Pygmalion and Galatea, 46

Quarterly Review, 6-7, 24

Railo, Eino, 10-11, 51
Rao, E. Nageswara, 22
Rieger, James, 14-15, 29
　magic in *Frankenstein,* 51
　text of *Frankenstein,* 1
Ritter, Johann Wilhelm, 78-79
Robertson, Etienne-Gaspard
　magic lantern of, 71, 72
robot, 48-50
Rossetti, Lucy Maddox, 8

secret doctrine, 58ff.
Shelley, Mary
　knowledge of contemporary science, 72-75, 77
Shelley, Percy Bysshe
　Alastor, 22
　chemistry, 77
　Prometheus Unbound, 1
Small, Christopher, 27-29
solar microscope, 72
Spark, Muriel, 12
speculative fiction, 2, 14, 23, 24, 25, 26-27, 28, 82
Swingle, L.J., 62

Temple of Nature, 27
Thomas, Mrs., 32
Thousand Nights and One Night, 46
Trembley, Abraham, 24

Walling, William A., 29